EMMA MAXWELL

Financial Freedom Made Easy

Copyright © 2024 by Emma Maxwell

All rights reserved. No part of this publication may be reproduced, stored or transmitted in any form or by any means, electronic, mechanical, photocopying, recording, scanning, or otherwise without written permission from the publisher. It is illegal to copy this book, post it to a website, or distribute it by any other means without permission.

Emma Maxwell asserts the moral right to be identified as the author of this work.

Emma Maxwell has no responsibility for the persistence or accuracy of URLs for external or third-party Internet Websites referred to in this publication and does not guarantee that any content on such Websites is, or will remain, accurate or appropriate.

First edition

This book was professionally typeset on Reedsy.
Find out more at reedsy.com

Contents

Introduction	vi
Chapter 1	1
Foundations of Financial Literacy	1
1.1 Understanding Your Financial Mindset	1
1.2 The Importance of Financial Literacy for Families	3
1.3 Breaking Down Financial Jargon	5
1.4 Setting Realistic Financial Goals	6
1.5 The Basic Principles of Budgeting	8
1.6 Creating a Family Financial Plan	10
Chapter 2	13
Mastering Budgeting and Saving Techniques	13
2.1 Crafting a Monthly Family Budget	13
2.2 Identifying and Reducing Unnecessary Expenses	15
2.3 Strategies for Saving on Everyday Purchases	20
2.4 Building an Emergency Fund on a Tight Budget	22
2.5 Automating Savings to Ensure Consistency	24
2.6 Utilizing Budgeting Apps for Financial Management	25
Chapter 3	29
Debt Management and Elimination Strategies	29
3.1 Understanding Different Types of Debt	29
3.2 The Debt Pay Down Method: Small Wins, Big Payoffs	31
3.3 The Debt Accelerator Method: Reducing Interest Costs	33
3.4 Dealing with Credit Card Debt Effectively	35
3.5 Strategies for Managing Student Loans	37
3.6 Avoiding Common Debt Traps	39
Chapter 4	42

Investing Basics for Families	42
4.1 Introduction to Investing: Why It Matters	42
4.2 Understanding Stocks, Bonds, and Mutual Funds	44
4.3 The Power of Compound Interest	46
4.4 Diversifying Your Investment Portfolio	47
4.5 Investing in Low-Cost Index Funds	50
4.6 Setting Up a Family Investment Plan	51
Chapter 5	54
Retirement Planning Essentials	54
5.1 Calculating Your Retirement Needs	54
5.2 Understanding Different Retirement Accounts	56
5.3 Strategies for Long-Term Retirement Savings	58
5.4 Balancing Retirement Savings with Other Financial Goals	60
5.5 Avoiding Common Retirement Planning Mistakes	62
5.6 Ensuring a Comfortable Retirement Lifestyle	64
Chapter 6	68
Financial Education for Children	68
6.1 Age-Appropriate Financial Lessons for Kids	68
6.2 Fun, Interactive Exercises for Teaching Money Skills	71
6.3 Encouraging Savings Habits in Young Children	72
6.4 Introducing Investment Concepts to Teens	74
6.5 Resources and Tools for Family Financial Education	76
Chapter 7	79
Tax Planning and Maximizing Savings	79
7.1 Understanding Your Tax Bracket	79
7.2 Utilizing Tax-Advantaged Accounts	81
7.3 Strategies for Minimizing Tax Liabilities	83
7.4 Planning for Tax Season	84
7.5 Common Tax Deductions and Credits for Families	86
7.6 Long-term Tax Planning Strategies	89
Chapter 8	91
Overcoming Psychological Barriers and Building Wealth	91
8.1 Recognizing Psychological Barriers to Financial Success	91

8.2 Developing a Healthy Money Mindset	93
8.3 Overcoming Fear and Anxiety About Money	95
8.4 Building Financial Confidence Through Education	97
8.5 Creating a Wealth-Building Routine	99
8.6 Celebrating Financial Milestones and Progress	101
Conclusion	105
References	109

Introduction

Think about this: a parent sits at the kitchen table, surrounded by a mountain of bills. They wonder how they'll pay for everything on time and still save for their child's college education. This moment of feeling overwhelmed is all too common. Many families face financial struggles, and it's not because they don't work hard. It's often because they never learned the basics of managing money at school.

Hi, I'm Emma, a CPA-qualified accountant. Believe it or not, I never learned financial basics at school. When my son was born, I realized I needed to get my act together. I wanted to make solid financial decisions for my family. So, I went on a learning journey to better myself. Through trial and error, I've learned a lot, and now I want to share what I've discovered with you.

The purpose of this book is simple: to teach you basic financial principles and show you how to manage your money effectively. You don't need to feel overwhelmed. These principles are easy to learn and apply. Whether you're dealing with debt or trying to save for the future, this book will help you improve your family's financial situation.

Financial literacy is crucial for everyone. Did you know that a significant percentage of people don't have an emergency fund or a budget? According to research, many families struggle because they were never taught how to handle money. A recent Customer Research Report showed that people seek financial planning books because they want to fill this gap in their education. Schools often don't teach these principles, but it's never too late to learn.

So, what will you gain from this book? Here are the key takeaways:

- Understanding debt and how you can pay it down
- Creating and maintaining a budget

- Knowing where your money goes
- Building an emergency fund
- Basics of Investing
- Saving for college
- Planning for retirement
- Understanding tax basics
- How to have a great money mindset

These are practical, actionable steps that you can take to improve your finances. You'll find that these principles are not just theory. They're real solutions that can make a difference in your life.

Throughout the book, I'll share real-life examples from my own experiences. You'll also read stories of other families who have successfully managed their finances. These stories make the advice relatable and credible. You'll see that you're not alone in your struggles and that success is possible.

The book is structured logically, starting with the basics and moving on to more advanced topics. Here's a brief overview of the chapters:

1. Introduction to Financial Literacy
2. Budgeting Basics
3. Managing Debt
4. The Basics of Investing
5. Planning for Retirement
6. Teaching your Kids about Money
7. The Basics of Tax
8. Money Mindset and Building Lasting Wealth

Each chapter will end with specific, actionable steps you can take to improve your financial situation right away. You'll have a clear path to follow, making it easier to take control of your financial future.

I encourage you to take the first step toward financial freedom and stability for your family. You have the power to change your financial situation. With the right knowledge and tools, you can build a better future. So, let's get started on this journey together. Your financial freedom journey starts now.

Chapter 1

Foundations of Financial Literacy

One evening, after putting the kids to bed, you sit down with a cup of tea and a stack of bills. The numbers don't add up, and you feel a knot in your stomach. You wonder how others manage to save for college, pay off debt, and still have money left for a family vacation. The truth is, that many people feel the same way. Financial literacy is not just about knowing how to budget or invest; it's also about understanding your financial mindset.

1.1 Understanding Your Financial Mindset

Your financial mindset is the set of attitudes and beliefs you hold about money. These attitudes shape your financial behavior, often without you even realizing it. If you grew up constantly hearing that money was scarce, you might be overly cautious with spending or fearful of taking financial risks. On the other hand, if you were raised in an environment where money was freely spent, you might struggle with saving and budgeting. Our upbringing and cultural backgrounds play a significant role in shaping these beliefs. For example, some cultures emphasize frugality and saving, while others might prioritize enjoying the present moment, sometimes at the expense of future financial security.

Personal experiences also leave a lasting impact on how we view money. A person who has experienced financial hardship may develop a scarcity mindset, always worrying that there will never be enough. Conversely, someone who has seen the benefits of wise investments might adopt an abundance mindset, believing that there are always opportunities to grow wealth. These mindsets—scarcity and abundance—can significantly influence how we make financial decisions. A scarcity mindset often leads to excessive saving and risk aversion, while an abundance mindset can encourage calculated risks and long-term planning. Don't worry, mindsets can change once we know where we're starting from.

Recognizing and addressing negative financial beliefs is crucial for breaking free from limiting behaviors. Start by identifying these beliefs. Ask yourself questions like, "Do I believe that money is inherently hard to come by?" or "Do I think that I'll never be able to save enough?" Self-assessment tools, like financial behavior quizzes, can help you pinpoint these negative thoughts. Once identified, challenge these beliefs by reframing them. For instance, if you believe that investing is too risky, research and educate yourself on low-risk investment options. It's also essential to understand that failure is part of the learning process. If you've made financial mistakes before, don't let them define your future. Instead, use them as learning opportunities to build a stronger financial foundation.

Adopting a growth mindset towards finances can transform your financial situation. A growth mindset embraces learning and improvement, acknowledging that skills and knowledge can be developed over time. Consider the story of Jamie, a single mom who was drowning in debt. By changing her mindset and viewing each financial setback as a lesson, she gradually paid off her debt and built a savings cushion. Practical exercises, such as setting small, achievable financial goals or keeping a journal of your financial progress, can help develop this mindset.

To foster a healthier relationship with money, you could incorporate daily affirmations and positive money habits into your routine. Start your day with affirmations like, "I am capable of managing my finances effectively," or

CHAPTER 1

"Every dollar I save brings me closer to my goals." It has been proven that saying goals out loud increases your chances of goal success by 70%. If doing affirmations isn't your thing, writing goals down does make a big difference. Set small, achievable financial goals to build confidence. For example, aim to save $50 a month or reduce your dining-out expenses by $25. These small wins add up over time and boost your confidence. Surround yourself with others who can keep you accountable. Join a financial literacy group or find a mentor who can offer guidance and support. Don't feel that you'll be frowned upon as all these people started where you are at one point in their lives. Their encouragement can be invaluable as you work towards your financial goals.

Understanding your financial mindset is the first step toward financial literacy. By recognizing and addressing negative beliefs, adopting a growth mindset, and incorporating positive habits, you can transform your financial mindset. This chapter lays the foundation for the rest of the book, guiding you through practical steps to manage your money effectively and build a secure financial future for your family.

1.2 The Importance of Financial Literacy for Families

Financial literacy is a cornerstone for family well-being. Imagine a household where every financial decision leads to arguments and stress. This scenario is common and often stems from a lack of financial knowledge. When families understand money management, they experience less stress and conflict. Knowing how to budget, save, and invest can transform a household from a place of anxiety to one of stability and peace. Financial literacy equips everyone in the family to make informed decisions, reducing misunderstandings and fostering a collaborative environment.

Informed financial decisions contribute to long-term family stability. When parents have the skills to manage money wisely, they can plan for the future, ensuring that their children have access to education and opportunities. This stability is not just about having enough money, but about creating a secure environment where everyone feels confident about their financial future. It also means breaking the cycle of financial mismanagement that often passes from generation to generation. By educating ourselves, we can change the narrative for our children, teaching them the skills they need to thrive financially.

Financial literacy benefits different family members in unique ways. For parents, it means empowerment. They can make choices that align with their values and goals, whether it's saving for a family vacation or investing in a college fund. Financial literacy gives parents the tools to navigate life's financial challenges with confidence. For children, learning about money management from a young age sets them up for success. They develop essential skills that will serve them throughout their lives, from understanding the value of saving to making informed spending decisions. Extended family members, like grandparents, can also benefit. They might be involved in helping with family finances or setting up trusts and savings accounts for their grandchildren.

Statistics underscore the importance of financial literacy. For instance, more than 77 million Americans do not pay their bills on time, and 41% do not have a savings account. These numbers illustrate the widespread financial challenges that families face. Education can change this. Studies show that families who engage in financial literacy programs are better equipped to handle their finances and achieve long-term stability. The Financial Educators Council reports that financial literacy skills can lift families out of poverty and set them up for success. This is not just about dollars and cents; it's about creating a foundation for a better life.

Consider the story of the Jones family. They were drowning in debt and constantly stressed about money. They decided to take a financial literacy course together, learning how to budget, save, and invest. Over time, they paid off their debt, built an emergency fund, and even saved for a down payment on a house. Their journey was not easy, but it shows the transformative power of financial education. Another example is Jane, a single mother who struggled financially after a divorce. By educating herself on personal finance, she managed to turn her situation around, securing a stable future for herself and her children.

Financial literacy impacts the entire family unit. It reduces stress and conflict, contributes to long-term stability, and breaks generational cycles of financial mismanagement. It empowers parents to make informed decisions and teaches children essential money management skills. Statistics highlight the widespread need for financial education, and real-life examples show its positive outcomes. By embracing financial literacy, families can build a secure and prosperous future together.

1.3 Breaking Down Financial Jargon

When it comes to managing your money, it can feel like you're navigating a sea of confusing terms and concepts. Let's break down some of the key financial jargon you need to know, starting with "compound interest." Compound interest is the interest earned on both the initial principal and the interest that has been added to it. Think of it as a snowball effect: if you roll a small snowball down a hill, it picks up more snow and grows larger. Similarly, the longer you let your money sit in an account earning compound interest, the more it will grow over time. This concept is crucial for savings and investments, as it can significantly increase your wealth over the long term.

"P&I" stands for principal and interest. When you take out any type of loan, you repay both the principal (the original amount borrowed) and the interest (the cost of borrowing the money). Understanding the difference between principal and interest is crucial for managing loans effectively. For instance, in the early years of a mortgage, a larger portion of your payments goes toward interest. Knowing this can help you make informed decisions about refinancing or making extra payments to reduce the principal faster.

Inflation is another important term to understand. Inflation is the rate at which the general level of prices for goods and services rises, eroding the purchasing power of money. For example, if the inflation rate is 3%, a loaf of bread that costs $1 today will cost $1.03 next year. Inflation can impact your savings and investments, as the value of your money decreases over time. This is why it's essential to invest your money in assets that can grow faster than inflation, such as stocks or real estate.

Lastly, let's discuss "asset allocation." Asset allocation is the process of dividing your investments among different asset categories, such as stocks, bonds, and cash. The goal is to balance risk and reward according to your financial goals, risk tolerance, and your investment horizon. For example, a young investor with a long time until retirement might have a higher allocation to stocks, which offer higher potential returns but also higher risk. In contrast, someone nearing retirement might allocate more to bonds, which are generally safer but offer lower returns. Proper asset allocation can help you achieve your financial goals while managing risk.

Understanding these terms is not just about expanding your vocabulary. It's about making better financial decisions. For instance, knowing how compound interest works can motivate you to start saving early. Understanding P&I can help you manage your loans more effectively. Being aware of inflation can guide your investment choices, and knowing about asset allocation can help you build a diversified and resilient portfolio.

By breaking down financial jargon, we demystify the world of personal finance. Understanding these terms can empower you to make informed decisions, avoid costly mistakes, and take control of your financial future. Remember, financial literacy is a journey, and every step you take brings you closer to financial freedom and stability for your family.

1.4 Setting Realistic Financial Goals

Setting realistic financial goals is a foundational step in financial planning. Imagine trying to navigate without a map; you'd likely get lost or take much longer to reach your destination. Financial goals act as your roadmap, providing direction and motivation. When you have specific, measurable targets, it's easier to stay focused and motivated. Specific goals give you a clear vision, making it easier to track progress and maintain accountability. For example, instead of saying, "I want to save money," a specific goal would be, "I want to save $5,000 for a family vacation in one year." This specificity turns a vague desire into a concrete target.

To set effective financial goals, use the SMART criteria: Specific, Measurable, Achievable, Relevant, and Time-bound. Specific goals are clear and precise, like saving for a new car. Measurable goals allow you to track progress, such as saving $200 a month. Achievable goals are realistic given your circumstances, like cutting down on dining out to save more. Relevant goals align with your broader financial plans, ensuring they contribute to your overall well-being. Time-bound goals have a set timeframe, like saving $5,000 in two years. For instance, a SMART goal for a family could be, "Save $10,000 for a home down payment in three years by saving $278 monthly." Worksheets for setting and tracking these goals can be invaluable, helping you break down larger goals into smaller, manageable steps.

Common pitfalls in goal-setting can derail your financial plans. One significant mistake is setting unrealistic expectations. Perhaps you've aimed to save an unattainable amount in a short period. Managing such expectations involves being honest about your current financial situation and what is feasible. Another common error is setting goals without a clear plan of action. It's not enough to say, "I want to get out of debt." You need a detailed strategy, like paying off high-interest debt first. Once you've finished the first few chapters come back and revisit these goals and see if they're realistic or they've changed. Or you can do this on your monthly money nights. Not dedicating time to work toward your goals can also be a stumbling block. Consistency is key. Regularly setting aside time to review and adjust your plans ensures you stay on track.

Achieving financial goals requires practical strategies. Breaking down large goals into smaller, manageable steps makes them less daunting. For example, if your goal is to save $10,000 in two years, focus on saving $417 each month. Visual reminders, like charts or progress trackers, can keep you motivated. Place these in visible spots, like your fridge or smartphone. It's also important to remember that asking for help is not a sign of weakness. Whether it's consulting a financial advisor or joining a financial literacy group, seeking guidance can provide new insights and keep you accountable. Having an accountability group or a mentor can be incredibly beneficial. They can offer support, share their experiences, and keep you on track.

Setting realistic financial goals gives you a clear roadmap, making your financial journey manageable and less stressful. Remember, it's about progress, not perfection. Surround yourself with supportive individuals who can help you stay accountable, and don't be afraid to seek professional advice when needed.

Once you've brainstormed all your goals then write next to them the dates you want to achieve them by, if you haven't already. Then order them in date order, soonest goal first and then future goals later. You might want to pay down debt before you take that vacation to Disney World. Share these with your spouse - are you on the same page? If you're both running towards the same goals, great, if you're not then talk about it and agree on the order preference and deadlines. Don't be afraid to put some big goals on there like going to get your Masters at college in five years time; we'll work out how in Chapter 2.

1.5 The Basic Principles of Budgeting

Budgeting is like having a roadmap for your finances. Without it, you might find yourself lost, wondering where all your money went at the end of the month. The purpose of budgeting is to help you manage your finances effectively, ensuring that every dollar has a purpose. A well-crafted budget can be the key to achieving financial stability. When you know exactly how much money is coming in and going out, you can make informed decisions about spending and saving. This clarity not only helps in paying bills on time but also in setting aside money for future goals like vacations, college funds, or retirement.

The role of budgeting in reducing financial stress cannot be overstated.

CHAPTER 1

When you have a clear plan for your money, it alleviates the anxiety of unexpected expenses or looming bills. It improves decision-making by providing a framework within which you can evaluate your spending choices. For example, if your budget allocates $100 for dining out each month, you'll think twice before splurging on an expensive meal. Knowing your financial boundaries allows you to enjoy life without the constant worry of overspending.

There are several budgeting methods to choose from, each with its own set of advantages and disadvantages. The envelope system involves allocating cash into physical envelopes for different categories like groceries, entertainment, and utilities. Once the money in an envelope is spent, you can't spend any more in that category until the next month. This method is excellent for those who need a tangible way to control their spending but can be cumbersome in our increasingly cashless society. Zero-based budgeting, on the other hand, requires you to assign every dollar a job, ensuring that your income minus expenses equals zero. This approach is highly effective for those who want to ensure every penny is accounted for, but it requires meticulous planning and tracking. Percentage-based budgeting, such as the 50/30/20 rule, allocate 50% of your income to necessities, 30% to discretionary spending, and 20% to savings and debt repayment. This method is straightforward and flexible, but may not be detailed enough for those with complex financial situations.

Creating a budget starts with listing all your income sources, including salaries, freelance work, child support, and any other revenue streams. Next, list your expenses, dividing them into fixed (rent, utilities, loan payments) and variable (groceries, entertainment, dining out). Once you have a clear picture of your income and expenses, allocate funds to different categories based on your priorities and goals. Tools like spreadsheets or budgeting apps can simplify this process, allowing you to track and adjust your budget in real-time. Apps like Empower or Rocket Money offer user-friendly interfaces and features like automatic expense categorization and goal tracking.

Maintaining and adjusting your budget is crucial for its effectiveness. Life is unpredictable, and your financial situation can change due to unexpected expenses, job changes, or shifts in priorities. Regularly reviewing your budget allows you to make necessary adjustments, ensuring it remains relevant and effective. Set aside time each month to go over your income and expenses, identifying areas where you might need to cut back or where you can afford to allocate more funds. Flexibility is key; a budget should be a living document that evolves with your financial landscape.

For example, if you receive a raise at work, you might decide to increase your savings contributions or pay down debt faster. On the flip side, if an unexpected medical bill arises, you may need to temporarily reduce discretionary spending to cover the cost. Budgeting apps can be particularly helpful in maintaining this flexibility. Many of these tools offer features like automatic updates, spending alerts, and customizable categories, making it easier to stay on top of your finances. A simple spreadsheet can also do the trick, allowing you to manually input and adjust your figures as needed.

Budgeting is not just about restricting spending; it's about making informed choices that align with your financial goals. By understanding the purpose and importance of budgeting, exploring different methods, and following a step-by-step process to create and maintain your budget, you can achieve greater financial stability and peace of mind. Remember, a budget is a tool to help you take control of your finances, reduce stress, and make better decisions for your family's future.

1.6 Creating a Family Financial Plan

Creating a family financial plan is like building a house. You need a solid foundation and all the essential components to ensure it stands strong. A comprehensive financial plan includes several key elements: budgeting, saving, investing, and insurance. Each element plays a crucial role in securing your financial future. Budgeting helps you manage your day-to-day expenses. Saving ensures you have a cushion for emergencies and future goals. Investing allows your money to grow over time, and insurance protects you against unforeseen events. Short-term goals might include saving for a vacation or paying off a credit card, while long-term goals could be buying a home or planning for retirement.

Involving the entire family in financial planning is vital. It creates a sense of shared responsibility and ensures everyone is on the same page. Consider holding regular family monthly Money meetings to discuss financial goals and progress. This can be a relaxed affair, perhaps a budget date night with a bottle of wine for couples or a family gathering with snacks and a game for the kids. These meetings can make financial planning less daunting and more engaging. Assigning financial responsibilities to different family members can also be helpful. For example, one person might track expenses while another handles savings and investments. This collaborative approach not only distributes the workload but also fosters a team spirit.

The benefits of having a financial plan are immense. A well-thought-out plan can lead to financial stability and peace of mind. For instance, the Johnson family used a financial plan to pay off their debt, build an emergency fund, and save for their children's education. By following their plan, they managed to reduce financial stress and improve their overall quality of life. A financial plan also helps mitigate risks by preparing you for unexpected events. Whether it's a medical emergency or a sudden job loss, having a plan in place ensures you're not caught off guard. It provides a safety net, allowing you to navigate life's uncertainties with confidence.

Moreover, a financial plan helps you stay focused on your long-term goals. It's easy to get sidetracked by short-term desires, but a plan reminds you of what's truly important. It keeps you accountable and motivated to stay the course. For example, if your goal is to save for a home, your plan will outline the steps you need to take, such as cutting back on discretionary spending and increasing your savings rate. This clarity can make a significant difference in your financial journey, helping you achieve your dreams faster.

Involving the entire family in the process through regular meetings and assigned responsibilities can foster a sense of shared commitment. Practical tools like templates and worksheets can simplify the planning process. The benefits of a financial plan include financial stability, reduced stress, and the ability to navigate life's uncertainties with confidence. By having a clear plan, you can stay focused on your long-term goals and achieve financial peace of mind.

Don't move on to the next chapter without doing the following;

1. Find a goal-setting worksheet or go old school and write your goals down on paper
2. Rank them in order from soonest goal to longest goal
3. Have a money night to all compare your goals so that you're on the same page before moving on

Chapter 2

Mastering Budgeting and Saving Techniques

Picture this: it's the end of the month, and you find yourself frantically checking your bank account, wondering how you spent so much money. The kids need new school supplies, the car is due for maintenance, and the holidays are just around the corner. This scenario is all too familiar for many families. The good news is that creating a monthly family budget can transform this chaos into a manageable, stress-free routine. A budget isn't just a list of numbers; it's a plan that helps you understand where every dollar goes, prioritize your spending, and save for the future.

2.1 Crafting a Monthly Family Budget

Creating a monthly family budget is essential for achieving financial stability. Think of it as a financial roadmap that guides you through the month, ensuring you know exactly where your money is going. One of the biggest benefits of having a budget is the clarity it provides. When you know where every dollar goes, you're in control. This knowledge helps you prioritize spending, ensuring that essential expenses are covered before you allocate money to non-essential items. For instance, you might realize that you're spending too much on dining out, which could be redirected toward building an emergency fund or paying down debt.

The first step in crafting a monthly family budget is listing all your income sources. This isn't just about your salary. Be sure to account for every possible source of income, including freelance work, child support, government benefits, and any side gigs. For example, if you drive for a ride-sharing service or sell handmade crafts online, that income should be included. Knowing your total income gives you a clear picture of what you have to work with each month, making it easier to allocate funds appropriately.

Next, identify your fixed and variable expenses. Fixed expenses are those that remain the same each month, such as your rent or mortgage, utilities, insurance, and car payments. These are the non-negotiables that you must pay to keep your household running smoothly. On the other hand, variable expenses can fluctuate from month to month. These include groceries, entertainment, dining out, and those often-overlooked cash purchases. Tracking these expenses might reveal areas where you can cut back. For example, if you notice that you're spending a significant amount on takeout, you might decide to cook more meals at home.

Balancing your income and expenses is crucial to avoid deficits. Start by comparing your total income with your total expenses. If your expenses exceed your income, it's time to make some adjustments. One effective technique for reallocating funds to cover essential expenses is the 50/30/20 rule. Allocate 50% of your income to needs, 30% to wants, and 20% to savings or debt repayment. This method provides a balanced approach to managing your finances, ensuring that you're covering your essentials while still setting aside money for the future.

When it comes to cutting non-essential spending, start small. Look for easy wins, like reducing your dining-out budget or canceling unused subscriptions. These small changes can add up over time, freeing up money that can be redirected toward more important goals. For instance, swapping a daily coffee shop visit for a home-brewed cup could save you hundreds of dollars a year. Additionally, consider negotiating better rates on fixed expenses like insurance or utilities. A simple phone call to your provider could result in significant savings.

To make this process easier, consider using a budgeting app or a simple spreadsheet. Apps like Empower or Rocket Money can simplify tracking your income and expenses, offering features like automatic expense categorization and goal tracking. These apps provide a clear overview of your financial situation, making it easier to identify areas for improvement and stay on track with your budget.

Don't despair if you are underwater here; the first step is knowing where every penny is going, and then you can plan to fix it. If you have a negative connotation around the word budget, just think of it as the tool that helps you manage money. Seeing the numbers in front of you might be the first time you've seen it laid out for you. This makes it easy to take action and do something about it. Go through in detail your income and expenses and see if there are ways to either increase your income or decrease your expenses. If you're in debt we're trying to free up some cash so that you can immediately pay down debt or build your emergency fund. The first step is seeing it in front of you in black and white; now let's take action!

2.2 Identifying and Reducing Unnecessary Expenses

Tracking your spending habits is the first step in identifying and reducing unnecessary expenses. Imagine this: for one month, you meticulously write down every penny you spend. This might seem tedious, but it's incredibly revealing and necessary. Use a spending diary to record each purchase, whether it's a cup of coffee or a quick grocery run. Analyzing bank and credit card statements can also help you see where your money is going. These statements provide a comprehensive overview of your spending patterns, allowing you to categorize expenses and spot trends that might not be obvious day-to-day.

Once you start tracking, you'll likely identify common areas where families typically overspend. Subscription services are a big one. It's easy to sign up for multiple streaming platforms, magazines, or fitness apps, but these can add up quickly. Next, impulse purchases are another culprit. Whether it's a tempting sale or an unplanned trip to the store, these small buys can significantly impact your budget. Dining out frequently is also a major expense. While the occasional meal out is fine, making it a habit can drain your wallet. These areas are often the easiest to overlook but can make a significant difference when addressed.

After you have analyzed a typical month of expenses, review your numbers. Where are you spending the most money? Often it's in housing, which by its nature is a fixed expense, but is it really? If you are renting, you could ask your landlord for a better weekly rent if you sign up to a longer lease. Or you might cut the grass or maintain the pool so they don't need to, and in appreciation, they might lower your rent. If you have a mortgage, there's no reason why you can't ring your bank to ask for a discount. If you are on a variable loan repayment, there are options. Check out NerdWallet which compares rates from different lenders. It asks you for your postcode and then comes up with the best options in that area. It lists the interest rate and the Annual Percentage Rate which is your interest rate including any fees on the loan like monthly account keeping fees or loan setup fees. Compare this to what you are currently paying - are they massively different? If they are, do the math on if you were to get that interest rate what your monthly repayments would decrease by. If it's a big difference, it's time for a phone call to your bank. Before you call your bank you need to be in good standing on your loan with income coming in and payments made on time. Your call will go something like this. "Hello bank, I would like to speak with your retention department as I am thinking about canceling my home loan and refinancing to a bank that will offer me a better rate." They may try to solve your problem themselves, but be firm and ask for a transfer. When you are connected to the retention department try something like this, "Hello bank, I have been a customer at this bank for (insert number of years) and have always liked banking here, but I have just done my homework and if I switch to (insert the banks name you're comparing to on NerdWallet) I can get an interest rate of (quote interest rate) which is substantially different from what I am getting with you. I wanted to allow you to match this rate; otherwise, I think I'm going to have to refinance with them as it's a substantial saving. They will offer you a discount, but initially, they won't come all the way down, so keep pushing. "I appreciate you coming down by 0.5% but the rate they're offering would be a 1.5% difference so unless you can match that I will refinance with the other bank." Again they will come down but potentially not all the way; keep pushing. They don't want to lose you, and you are speaking to someone who is authorized to make a deal, so keep going. I hope you save a heap of money doing this, I've had clients do this and save themselves thousands of dollars a year.

If your mortgage is on a fixed interest rate this is not possible until the end of your fixed term. They will not change your interest rate whilst you are on a fixed term, but once you come off fixed, there is a little wiggle room there. But if when you review interest rates on NerdWallet your rate is substantially different from that which is being offered in the market it might be worth doing the math on whether you should break this loan and refinance to something else. This, in most cases, will result in a break fee which can be substantial depending on how early into your loan you are. You may be able to get your new bank to cover this and wrap it into your new loan costs, or you may have to pay this in cash to break the loan. Don't despair yet, keep going as the monthly savings may be substantial. If your new interest rate might save you $1,000 a month, and it costs $5,000 to break the loan, then it will be worth it in the long run. Do your homework and speak to a good mortgage broker who can help you out. Your mortgage broker should not be from the same bank you bank with, they should be able to offer you loans from multiple lenders on their panel so that you have many options to compare.

Other fixed expenses are utilities, car loans, and insurance. You should set aside 15 minutes for each of these phone calls and do the same thing as you did with your home loan. Ask your utility provider if they have any pay-on-time discounts, or if they can lower your rate. Likewise with your car loan, are they able to reduce your interest rate or monthly repayments? Do not lengthen the loan to reduce your monthly repayments unless you are really strapped for money, as all that does is continue your repayments for longer and we want that debt paid as soon as possible. Do you need an expensive car loan payment every month? Or could you just buy a cheaper car outright and upgrade to a more expensive car when you're financially able. For insurance, pull out all of your insurance policies and use a comparison calculator to compare if you're getting a good deal. Type into Google car insurance, and you should be able to compare your car insurance to other providers. Check if you're getting a good deal or if it's time to switch. Again, call the retention department and ask for a better deal as you're looking at moving somewhere else to save money. Home and contents insurance seems to just keep going up and up, and you seem to get penalized for a tornado that ripped through people's houses on the other side of the country, but never fear, a call to their call center could save you thousands. Tell them you are looking to save some money on your premium and that you are prepared to move elsewhere, and you should see some reductions in monthly premiums.

I hope some of these tips have saved you money. Don't accept no for an answer and keep pressing. Also, don't be afraid to make these phone calls, as they will save you money, and that goes straight to your wallet. It could help save for a vacation or to pay down debt. It's better off in your pocket, so go on, you can do it!

Then analyze your variable expenses. Look at what you're spending in each area and do a review. Are your expenses higher than your monthly income? Well, then this is a problem and may be why you're living on credit cards. Your expenses are staring back at you in black and white here, so it might be time to adjust some of these expenses down. If you're spending $1,000 a month on groceries and also spending $1,000 on dining out it might be too much. How much is your morning coffee run costing you? Can you make your coffee at home or brown bag your lunch a few days a week?

To cut down on these expenses, start by setting limits. For dining out, decide on a monthly budget less than what you're spending now and stick to it. Maybe allow yourself one or two meals out a month and plan meals at home for the rest. Canceling unused subscriptions is another straightforward way to save money. Go through and list all your subscriptions and ask yourself if you really use each one. If not, cancel it. Many services offer easy cancellation options online, and it's easy to just stream for a month at a time. Try having Netflix for one month and then Prime for another month. Another one I see a lot is gym subscriptions. Don't get me wrong, going to the gym is great if you're using it! If you're not using it, cancel it and try free apps like Nike Training Club or Caliber, or go for a walk outside. Cutting these out can free up funds for more important things, like savings or debt repayment.

Do this for a month, and then keep track of your expenses again the following month. How much did you save? We'll address what to do with this extra cash later on in the book, but good on you for taking action and saving money.

Understanding the psychological aspects of spending can also help you manage your finances better. Emotional triggers often drive unnecessary purchases. Perhaps you shop when you're stressed, hungry, or feeling down. Recognizing these triggers is the first step to overcoming them. Techniques for mindful spending can help you make more deliberate choices. For instance, before making a purchase, ask yourself if you truly need the item or if it's an emotional buy. Taking a moment to reflect can prevent impulse buys. Another technique is the 24-hour rule: wait a day before making a non-essential purchase. Often, the urge to buy will pass, saving you money.

By monitoring your daily expenditures, you gain a clearer understanding of your spending habits. Use tools like Rocket Money or a spending diary and analyze your bank and credit card statements to track where your money goes. Some of these apps actually link to your bank accounts and make the job easy for you to track. Identify areas where you typically overspend, such as subscription services, impulse purchases, and dining out frequently. Implement practical strategies to reduce these expenses, like setting limits on dining out and canceling unused subscriptions. Recognizing the psychological aspects of spending can further help you manage your finances. Understand your emotional triggers and adopt mindful spending techniques to make more deliberate financial decisions.

2.3 Strategies for Saving on Everyday Purchases

Smart shopping is a game-changer for any family looking to stretch their budget further. One of the best ways to make the most of your money is by comparing prices before making a purchase. Whether you're buying groceries, clothes, or electronics, it pays to shop around. Websites like PriceGrabber and Google Shopping can help you compare prices across different retailers, ensuring you get the best deal. Additionally, keeping an eye out for sales, special promotions, and discounts can save you a significant amount over time. Utilizing coupons and discount codes can also add up. Websites like RetailMeNot and PayPal Honey offer a plethora of codes for various online stores. Even a small discount can make a big difference when applied consistently. And don't forget about online specials and free delivery options. Services like Amazon Prime offer not only fast shipping but also access to exclusive deals and discounts. These small steps can collectively lead to substantial savings.

Another effective strategy is buying in bulk. Bulk buying can lead to significant savings, especially for items you use regularly, such as household supplies, non-perishable foods, and toiletries. Membership stores like Costco and Sam's Club offer bulk items at lower per-unit prices, making them a smart choice for families. For instance, purchasing a large pack of toilet paper or canned goods can be much cheaper per unit than buying smaller quantities frequently. However, it's essential to ensure that the items you buy in bulk are things you'll use before they expire. Otherwise, you might end up wasting money instead of saving it. Keep an eye out for bulk deals on items like pasta, rice, and cleaning supplies, which have a long shelf life and are used regularly.

Cashback and rewards programs are another excellent way to save on everyday purchases. Credit card rewards programs can offer cash back, points, or miles for every dollar spent. These rewards can be redeemed for statement credits, travel, or even gift cards. For instance, using a cashback credit card for groceries and gas can earn you a percentage back on every purchase, which adds up over time. Additionally, cashback apps like Rakuten and Honey can be used for online shopping. These apps provide a percentage of your purchase back as cash, which can be redeemed through PayPal or as a check. By stacking these rewards with sales and discounts, you can maximize your savings.

When it comes to saving on utilities and household expenses, there are several actionable steps you can take. Energy-saving practices can significantly reduce your monthly bills. Simple changes like switching to LED bulbs, using energy-efficient appliances, and unplugging devices when not in use can lead to substantial savings. I saved $1,000 per year by turning off my washing machine and dryer at the wall after I had finished each load and installing power-saving switches in my home. Additionally, consider negotiating better rates for services like internet, cell phone, and cable. Many providers are willing to offer discounts to retain customers. It's worth calling your service providers annually to ask for better rates or explore more affordable plans. Assess whether you still need a landline if you have a cell phone, as cutting this cost can save you money each month.

Another creative way to increase your income is by utilizing Airbnb. If you have extra space, consider renting out a room in your house. This can generate additional income that can be used to pay down your mortgage or other expenses. Similarly, if you travel frequently, renting out your home while you're away can help cover the costs of your trip.

Finally, consider taking on a roommate to share your house. This arrangement can significantly reduce your housing costs, making it easier to save for other financial goals. Sharing expenses like rent, utilities, and groceries can free up a substantial portion of your budget. It's essential to choose a roommate carefully to ensure compatibility and avoid potential conflicts. By taking these steps, you can make the most of your money, reduce unnecessary expenses, and build a more secure financial future for you and your family.

2.4 Building an Emergency Fund on a Tight Budget

Did you know that 68% of Americans don't have more than one month of expenses saved if they lost their job today? An emergency fund is a financial cushion that can give you peace of mind. Imagine dealing with unexpected medical bills, car repairs, a sudden job loss, or a leaky roof without the added stress of wondering how you'll pay for it. Having an emergency fund means you have a financial buffer for these unplanned expenses, allowing you to handle life's surprises without derailing your overall financial plan. It's about having the security to know that you can manage whatever comes your way without going into debt.

Starting small and building gradually is the key to creating an emergency fund, especially if you're on a tight budget. Even small savings can grow over time. Begin by setting aside a small amount each week. Think of it as paying yourself first. You might start with just $5 or $10 a week. While this may seem insignificant, it adds up. For instance, saving $10 a week translates to $520 a year. One effective method is to use spare change jars. Every time you get change, put it in a jar. At the end of the month, deposit this money into your emergency fund. It's surprising how quickly small amounts can accumulate.

Finding extra money to add to your fund can be easier than you think. Look around your home for items you no longer use or need. Selling unused items online can bring in extra cash. Platforms like eBay, Facebook Marketplace, or even local consignment shops are great places to start. Additionally, consider taking on a side gig or freelance work. Whether it's dog walking, babysitting, tutoring, or freelance writing, these extra jobs can boost your income. If your schedule allows, working additional hours at your current job can also provide extra funds. This extra income can be directly funneled into your emergency fund, accelerating its growth.

Deciding where to keep your emergency fund is crucial. The goal is to have quick access to your money when you need it, but you also want it to earn some interest. High-yield savings accounts are a great option. They offer better interest rates than regular savings accounts, allowing your money to grow faster while still being easily accessible. Many online banks offer high-yield savings accounts with competitive rates and no minimum balance requirements. Another option is money market accounts. These accounts also offer higher interest rates and come with check-writing privileges, making it easy to access your money if an emergency arises. Just ensure that you are going to meet their minimum deposit criteria; otherwise, you won't get the interest benefits.

Ensuring that your emergency fund is easily accessible but still earning interest is a smart financial move. High-yield savings accounts and money market accounts provide the best of both worlds. They keep your money safe while allowing it to grow. Remember, the purpose of an emergency fund is to be a financial safety net. It's not about earning high returns; it's about having the money available when you need it most. This is why I don't recommend investing this money in shares as if your water heater breaks down and you need immediate access to the money, you will have to sell down shares, which may be in a loss-making position.

Starting an emergency fund might seem daunting, especially if you're already stretched thin, but small steps can make a big difference. Begin by setting aside small amounts each week, and your money will grow over time. Look for creative ways to find extra money, such as selling unused items or taking on side gigs. Choose the right place to store your funds, like high-yield savings accounts or money market accounts, to ensure your money is both accessible and earning interest. If you have children you can involve them in the process by putting up a savings graph on the fridge, for instance, to save $1,000 and color it in each time you deposit money. I did this with my son when he was saving for a vacation and each time he put money into the fund we talked about it, congratulated him, and talked about how he was going to save the rest and by when.

2.5 Automating Savings to Ensure Consistency

Imagine setting up a system where your savings grow without you having to think about it. That's the beauty of automated savings. Automation can help in consistently building your savings by taking the effort and decision-making out of the equation. By setting up automatic transfers from your paycheck or bank account, you ensure that money is saved before you get a chance to spend it. This method leverages the principle of "paying yourself first," making saving as routine as paying your bills. Many families have found success with this approach, as it provides a hassle-free way to build their savings over time.

Setting up automatic transfers is straightforward and can often be done through your bank's online features. Start by logging into your online banking account and navigating to the section for setting up transfers. You can typically schedule these transfers to occur on specific dates, such as the day after your paycheck is deposited. This ensures that a portion of your income goes directly into a savings account before you can spend it. Additionally, there are apps like Raiz and Digit that can facilitate automatic savings. Raiz rounds up your purchases to the nearest dollar and invests the difference in a bank account or shares, while Oportun analyzes your spending habits and transfers small amounts of money you won't miss into a savings account. These tools make it easy to save without even realizing it.

Consistency in saving is crucial because regular, small contributions can grow significantly over time. The power of compound interest makes this possible. For example, if you save $100 a month with an annual interest rate of 5%, you'll see your savings grow to more than $6,800 in five years. The longer you leave the money to grow, the more it benefits from compound interest. This means that starting to save early, even in small amounts, can have a substantial impact on your financial future. Automating your savings ensures that these contributions happen regularly, without you having to remember to make the transfers each month.

Maintaining and adjusting automated savings is just as important as setting them up. It's a good idea to review your savings goals periodically to ensure they still align with your financial situation and objectives. If you receive a raise at work, consider increasing the amount you automatically transfer into savings. This way, your savings grow in proportion to your income. Regularly reviewing your automated savings ensures that they continue to meet your needs and goals. You might find that you can afford to save more or need to adjust your savings rate to account for changes in your expenses. Many banking apps and savings tools offer features that make it easy to adjust your transfer amounts and schedules.

Incorporating these practices into your financial routine can make a significant difference. Automated savings remove the temptation to skip saving in favor of immediate wants. They create a disciplined approach to building your emergency fund. With tools like online banking features and apps such as Raiz and Oportun, setting up and maintaining automatic savings has never been easier. Regularly reviewing and adjusting your savings ensures they keep pace with your financial growth. By making savings automatic, you ensure that you're consistently working towards your financial goals, building a secure future for your family without the stress of manual transfers each month.

2.6 Utilizing Budgeting Apps for Financial Management

In today's digital age, budgeting apps have become invaluable tools for families looking to manage their finances more effectively. These apps simplify the process of tracking income and expenses, setting financial goals, and staying on top of your budget. Among the most popular are Empower, YNAB (You Need A Budget), and EveryDollar. Each of these apps offers unique features tailored to different financial needs, making it easier for families to find one that suits their lifestyle.

Empower is a comprehensive financial tracking app that offers a range of features to help you manage your money. It connects to your bank accounts, credit cards, and other financial institutions, automatically categorizing your transactions. This means you can see all your finances in one place, making it easier to track spending and identify areas where you can save. Empower also offers budgeting tools, bill reminders, and even free credit score monitoring, giving you a complete picture of your financial health. It's an excellent choice for families looking for an all-in-one financial management tool and is currently free.

YNAB, or You Need A Budget, takes a different approach with its zero-based budgeting method. This means you allocate every dollar of your income to specific categories, ensuring that your income minus your expenses equals zero. YNAB's philosophy is to help you live on last month's income, which can be a game-changer for families trying to break the cycle of living paycheck to paycheck. The app offers real-time syncing across devices, allowing all family members to stay updated on the budget. It also provides educational resources to help you improve your financial literacy. YNAB is perfect for those who want a more hands-on approach to budgeting and are committed to making every dollar count. It does have a monthly subscription fee, currently $14.99 a month so be sure to factor that into your expenses.

EveryDollar, created by financial guru Dave Ramsey, is designed with simplicity in mind. It's particularly effective for families looking to get out of debt and anyone starting from scratch. The app uses a zero-based budgeting system but focuses heavily on debt payoff. You can set up personalized categories, track your spending, and see how much progress you're making on your debt repayment goals. The premium version even offers bank account syncing, making it easier to track your transactions. EveryDollar is ideal for families who are serious about debt elimination and want a straightforward, user-friendly budgeting tool. It is currently $12.99 a month.

Monarch Money is another robust option that offers comprehensive financial tracking. It allows you to add household members with separate log-ins, providing a shared financial dashboard that everyone can access. Monarch Money focuses on future goals and progress, helping families stay on track with their long-term financial plans. The app is ad-free and prioritizes security, ensuring your financial data is protected. Monarch Money is an excellent choice for families who want a collaborative approach to managing their finances and is currently $14.99 a month.

Credit Karma, while primarily known for tracking credit scores, also offers financial management tools. It provides insights into your credit health, helping you understand how your financial activities impact your credit score. The app offers personalized recommendations for improving your credit, as well as alerts for any significant changes. Credit Karma is a great supplement to a primary budgeting app, providing additional tools to help you maintain a healthy credit profile. It also has a great website that has comparison calculators for home loans and car loans.

Setting up these apps is straightforward and can significantly streamline your financial management. Start by downloading the app of your choice and creating an account. The next step is linking your bank accounts, credit cards, and other financial accounts. This allows the app to automatically import your transactions, saving you the hassle of manual entry. Once your accounts are linked, set up your budget categories. These might include groceries, utilities, entertainment, and savings. Most apps offer pre-set categories, but you can customize them to fit your family's unique needs.

Regularly reviewing your app data is crucial for staying on top of your finances. Schedule weekly check-ins to monitor your spending and ensure you're staying within your budget. These check-ins can be as simple as glancing at your app while enjoying your morning coffee. Monthly Money reviews are also essential. During these reviews, take a closer look at your spending patterns, adjust your budget categories if necessary, and review your goals. This ongoing engagement helps you stay accountable and make informed financial decisions. Try setting up a date night to review it or a dinner with the family, so everyone can stay involved and engaged. This is a great chance for you to teach your kids about financial responsibility, as they won't learn it at school!

Using budgeting apps can transform the way you manage your family's finances. Apps like Empower, YNAB, EveryDollar, Monarch Money, and Credit Karma offer unique features that cater to different financial needs. Setting up these apps involves linking your accounts and customizing budget categories, making the process seamless and efficient. Regularly reviewing your app data ensures you stay on track, allowing you to make adjustments and set new goals as needed. Embracing these digital tools can simplify financial management, giving you more control over your money and helping you achieve your financial goals. If you're not into digital apps, then go old school and track it in a spreadsheet or on paper; the key is regularly tracking and monitoring.

As we transition to the next chapter on managing debt, remember that budgeting is the foundation of financial stability. With a solid budget in place, you'll be better equipped to tackle other financial challenges and build a secure future for your family.

Don't move on to the next chapter without doing the following;

1. Listing your monthly expenses and income or set up one app to do so
2. Brainstorming ideas to increase your income
3. Look at ways to reduce your expenses if they are too big
4. Set a monthly budget and track it
5. Call your bank if you have a home loan to ask for a rate reduction if you have a variable-rate home loan
6. Investigate refinancing options with your mortgage broker if you have a fixed home loan including if there are any break fees
7. Call your utility provider to ask for a discount
8. Review your insurances and ring to ask for a discount
9. Set up automatic transfers from your online banking
10. Cancel some subscription services you no longer need or a costly gym membership
11. Set up a high-yield savings account if you don't already have one to put your emergency fund in

Come on, I know you can do it. These steps might take you a while but trust me these calls will be worth it.

Ok, now you've done the hard work, let's move on.

Chapter 3

Debt Management and Elimination Strategies

Picture this: you've just put the kids to bed, and as you sit down with a cup of tea, you pull out a stack of bills. The thought of sorting through them feels overwhelming. You're not alone. Debt can feel like a heavy weight, making it hard to see a way out. However, understanding the different types of debt and how to manage them can make a world of difference.

3.1 Understanding Different Types of Debt

Debt comes in many forms, and knowing the differences can help you tackle it more effectively. Let's start with secured debt. Secured debt requires you to put up an asset as collateral. This means if you don't repay the loan, the lender can take the asset. Common examples include mortgages and car loans. For instance, if you have a mortgage, your house is the collateral. If you default, the bank can foreclose on your home. Similarly, with a car loan, the vehicle itself secures the debt. Because there's less risk for the lender, secured loans often come with lower interest rates.

On the other hand, unsecured debt doesn't require collateral. These loans are issued based on your creditworthiness and your promise to repay. Credit cards, student loans, and personal loans are classic examples. With unsecured debt, there's no asset for the lender to seize if you default, which makes these loans riskier for lenders. As a result, they typically carry higher interest rates. For example, credit card debt can have interest rates upward of 20%, which can quickly add up if you're only making minimum payments.

Interest rates play a crucial role in the total cost of borrowing. High-interest debts, like credit cards and some car loans, can balloon out of control if not managed properly. Imagine you have a credit card balance of $5,000 with a 20% interest rate. If you only make minimum payments, it could take you years to pay off and cost you thousands in interest. In contrast, low-interest debts, such as student loans and home loans, cost you less over time. For instance, a home loan with a 4% interest rate is far more manageable and less expensive in the long run compared to high-interest debt.

Understanding which debts to prioritize is essential for effective debt management. Priority debts are those with the most severe consequences if not paid. Mortgages or rent should be at the top of your list. Missing these payments can lead to foreclosure or eviction, which is a crisis no family wants to face. Utility bills also fall into this category. Without paying these, you risk losing essential services like water, electricity, and heating. Taxes are another critical priority. Unpaid taxes can result in penalties, interest charges, and even legal action.

To keep track of your debt, it's helpful to use tools that can organize and categorize everything. A debt-tracking spreadsheet can be a simple yet powerful tool. Start by listing all your debts, including the creditor, balance, interest rate, and minimum payment. This visual representation helps you see the big picture and prioritize payments. Online tools and apps for debt management can also simplify this process. Apps like Debt Payoff Planner or Undebt.it can help you track your progress, set goals, and create a personalized repayment plan.

Organizing your debt is the first step towards taking control. By understanding the differences between secured and unsecured debt, recognizing the impact of high-interest versus low-interest debt, and identifying priority debts, you can create a clear plan of action. This approach helps you manage your current debt and sets the stage for financial stability and peace of mind moving forward. Paying down your debt is a priority and should be done whilst you start saving for your emergency fund.

I'm going to go through ways to help you pay down debt and hopefully get you debt-free sooner. These methods are;

- The Debt Pay Down Method: you pay down the smallest debt first
- The Debt Accelerator Method: you pay down the highest interest rate first
- Contacting your Debt Providers

3.2 The Debt Pay Down Method: Small Wins, Big Payoffs

When you're buried under a mountain of debt, it can feel impossible to see a way out. The Debt Pay Down Method offers a way to tackle that mountain one small step at a time. The idea is simple: you start by paying off your smallest debts first, regardless of the interest rates. This approach might seem counterintuitive, but it has powerful psychological benefits. Paying off the smallest debts first gives you quick wins, which can be incredibly motivating. These early victories build momentum and give you the confidence to tackle larger debts. It's like clearing the smaller hurdles first, making the bigger ones seem more manageable.

To implement the Debt Pay Down Method, start by listing all your debts from smallest to largest. This isn't just about numbers; it's about creating a clear plan of attack. Once you have your list, make minimum payments on all your debts except the smallest one. The reason you make all the minimum monthly payments is because if you don't, you also get slugged with a late fee or other fixed fees as well which just adds to your debt balance. So it is crucial that you make the minimum monthly payment and you make it on time every month. Focus all your extra funds on paying off this smallest debt. The idea is to knock it out as quickly as possible. Once it's paid off, take the money you were putting towards it and apply it to the next smallest debt on your list. Keep repeating this process. As you eliminate each debt, the amount you can put towards the next one grows, like a snowball rolling down a hill and gathering more snow.

Real-life examples can be incredibly inspiring when you're trying to pay off debt. Take Brian and Lindsey Allan, for instance. They used the Debt Pay Down Method to pay off $130,000 in student loans in just four years. They lived frugally, set a strict budget, and focused on their smallest debts first. Their story is a testament to the power of small wins and disciplined budgeting. Another example is the Smith family, who faced credit card, medical, and auto loan debts. By following the Debt Pay Down Method, they managed to pay off $50,000 in debt over three years. These stories show that it's possible to achieve financial freedom with determination and a clear plan.

To get started with the Debt Pay Down Method, you'll need some tools to help you stay organized and motivated. Debt pay-down calculators can be incredibly useful. These online tools allow you to input your debts and see a detailed plan for paying them off. They show you how long it will take to become debt-free and how much interest you'll save along the way. Printable tracking charts can also be a great resource. These charts let you visually track your progress, providing a tangible reminder of how far you've come. Place them somewhere visible, like on your fridge or next to your desk, to keep you motivated.

In addition to calculators and charts, consider using apps designed for debt management. Apps like Undebt.it and Debt Payoff Planner offer features tailored to the Debt Pay Down Method. They provide reminders, track your payments, and even offer motivational tips to keep you on track. These tools can simplify the process and make it easier to stay committed. Remember, the key to success with the Debt Pay Down Method is consistency. Make it a habit to review your debts and payments regularly. Celebrate each small win, and use that momentum to keep moving forward.

This is my least favorite of the three methods we'll talk about, but as mentioned, it has a really big psychological benefit when you have paid down one debt. By showing that you can do it, you use that momentum to keep going and pay down the next debt. In the Undebt.it app it has a Payoff Plan dashboard that shows based on each different payment method which strategy will pay down your debt fastest. Compare these methods to make an educated decision.

3.3 The Debt Accelerator Method: Reducing Interest Costs

When you're facing a mountain of debt, it's crucial to have a strategy that minimizes the financial burden. The Debt Accelerator Method focuses on paying off high-interest debt first, which can save you a significant amount of money over time. Unlike the Debt Pay Down Method, which prioritizes small wins by paying off the smallest debts first, the Debt Accelerator Method targets the debts that cost you the most in interest. This approach can lead to substantial financial benefits, as reducing interest costs allows more of your money to go toward paying down the principal balance.

To get started with the Debt Accelerator Method, begin by listing all your debts from highest to lowest interest rate. Your debts do not include your monthly car loan payment unless you have fallen behind in this payment. This list will be your roadmap. Make minimum payments on all your debts except the one with the highest interest rate. Apply any extra funds you have to this highest-interest debt. By focusing on the most expensive debt first, you reduce the overall interest you pay, which can expedite your journey to becoming debt-free. Once the highest-interest debt is paid off, move on to the next highest, continuing this process until all your debts are eliminated.

The long-term financial advantages of the Debt Accelerator Method are impressive. By paying off high-interest debts first, you reduce the total amount of interest you pay over the life of your loans. This can result in significant savings. For example, if you have $10,000 in credit card debt at a 20% interest rate, paying it off first can save you hundreds or even thousands of dollars compared to paying off lower-interest debts first. Comparison charts inside the Undebt.it app can show the different methods and how much you will pay down in each method, the total amount you'll pay, and when it will be paid off. Imagine two scenarios: one where you follow the Debt Pay Down Method and another where you use the Debt Accelerator Method. The total cost of debt and the time it takes to pay off everything can be dramatically different, with the Debt Accelerator Method often coming out ahead in terms of savings and speed.

Real-life success stories highlight the effectiveness of the Debt Accelerator Method. Take the case of the Carter family. They had multiple debts, including credit cards, a car loan, and student loans. By focusing on their highest-interest credit card debt first, they managed to save over $5,000 in interest payments. They started by making a list of all their debts, noting the interest rates and balances. They then focused all their extra funds on the credit card with the highest interest rate, while making minimum payments on the others. Once that debt was paid off, they moved to the next highest, eventually clearing all their debts much faster than they initially thought possible.

Another example is the Martinez family, who faced crippling credit card debt alongside a high-interest personal loan. They used the Debt Accelerator Method to tackle their debts strategically. By focusing on the personal loan first, which had a 25% interest rate, they avoided paying thousands in interest. After paying off the personal loan, they directed their efforts toward their credit card debt, which had a slightly lower interest rate. This method allowed them to pay off their debts in record time while saving a significant amount on interest.

To make the Debt Accelerator Method work for you, consider using tools that can help you stay organized and motivated. Debt payoff apps like Debt Payoff Planner or Undebt.it allow you to input your debts, interest rates, and minimum payments. These apps can calculate the optimal payment plan and show you how much interest you'll save over time. They also have visualization tools with progress charts, showing when your debt will be paid off. Watching your debt decrease and your interest savings grow can provide the encouragement you need to stick with the plan.

Implementing the Debt Accelerator Method requires discipline and consistency. Start by listing your debts from highest to lowest interest rate, make minimum payments on all but the highest-interest debt, and apply extra funds to that debt. The long-term financial benefits, including significant interest savings, make this method highly effective. Real-life success stories, like those of the Carter and Martinez families, demonstrate how powerful this strategy can be. This is the best way to pay down your debt, but be sure to include these minimum monthly debt payments into your budget that we addressed in Chapter 2.

3.4 Dealing with Credit Card Debt Effectively

High-interest credit card debt can quickly spiral out of control, causing significant financial stress. Imagine you have a $5,000 balance on a credit card with a 20% annual interest rate. If you only make minimum payments, it could take you over a decade to pay off, costing you thousands in interest. This is because minimum payments primarily cover interest and barely touch the principal. Over time, the interest accumulates, making your debt grow even if you're making regular payments. It's like trying to fill a bucket with a hole in it; no matter how much you pour in, it never seems to get full.

Okay, now I'm going to ask you to get uncomfortable. Yes, you'll be making phone calls again! Once you have your debt summary, which lists your debt, monthly minimum payments, and the interest rates on this debt, then we need to figure out a game plan. If you have a credit card with a high APR (Annual Percentage Rate) then we need to try and negotiate this. Do some research before you call on NerdWallet. Click on credit cards and then click on balance transfer. This will list the balance transfer credit cards available. This assumes you have good credit and can apply for this new card. You can either do two things - call your current credit card provider and ask for them to give you a rate reduction, or ask them to pause your interest rate. If they aren't interested in helping you out, then apply for this balance transfer card at 0% interest. This will reduce your payments right down to just paying off the principal with no interest. If you have bad credit then negotiating with your credit card provider is your only option, so be polite and tell them you understand you owe them money and want to work out how to do this in the fastest way but if they can help with reducing your interest rate that will help. They will likely help with reducing your interest rate if you have been making minimum monthly payments. If they can help update your APR and minimum payments, then input this into the debt spreadsheet that you are using or one of the apps.

If you end up getting a new balance transfer credit card, then once the balance has moved to the new credit card, cancel your old one and say goodbye to that card that got you into debt. Update the APR and minimum payments in the app that you are using to track your debt. It will then likely move your repayments to paying off other debt. This is a great move to decrease your monthly repayments and will ultimately make a massive difference in paying down your debt faster.

Another option is to roll your credit card debt into your home loan if you have equity. This can reduce the interest rate significantly, as home loans typically have much lower rates than credit cards. You will need to apply for an increase in your home loan, so you need to contact your bank or broker to organize this. Again, this relies on you having a good credit score and this process will take a little time to do as they may need a new valuation on your house and all the paperwork and approvals that are required. Please keep in mind that this will increase your home loan payments so make sure you put this increase into your monthly budget.

Changing spending habits is crucial to preventing future credit card debt. Cutting up or freezing your credit cards can help avoid the temptation to spend. If the cards are out of sight and hard to access, you're less likely to use them for non-essential purchases. Switching to a cash-only budget can also be a game-changer. When you use cash, you physically see the money leaving your hands, making you more mindful of your spending. Set a budget for categories like groceries, entertainment, and dining out. Withdraw the allocated amount in cash at the beginning of each month and commit to only spending what you have. This method may be a little harder in our cashless economy now.

To stay on track, utilize tools and resources designed for managing credit card debt. Credit card payoff calculators can be incredibly helpful. These tools let you input your balance, interest rate, and monthly payment to see how long it will take to pay off your debt. They can also show you how increasing your payments can shorten your repayment timeline and reduce the total interest paid. Budgeting apps like Empower are excellent for tracking credit card spending. These apps allow you to set budgets, categorize expenses, and monitor your spending in real time as we covered in Chapter 2. Seeing your spending patterns laid out can help you identify areas for improvement and stay within your budget.

Incorporating these strategies and tools can make a significant difference in managing and reducing credit card debt. By understanding the dangers of high-interest debt, adopting new spending habits, and utilizing practical tools, you can take control of your financial situation. This approach not only helps you pay off existing debt but also sets the stage for healthier financial habits moving forward.

3.5 Strategies for Managing Student Loans

Student loans can be a significant burden, but understanding the types of loans and repayment options available can make managing them more manageable. Federal loans and private loans are the two main types of student loans. Federal loans are issued by the government and come in several forms. Direct Subsidized Loans are need-based and have the government paying the interest while you're in school. Direct Unsubsidized Loans are not need-based, and you're responsible for all the interest, even while in school. PLUS Loans are available to graduate students and parents of undergraduates and have higher interest rates but offer larger borrowing limits. Private loans, on the other hand, are issued by banks, credit unions, or other financial institutions. They often have higher interest rates and stricter repayment terms. Understanding these differences is crucial when planning your repayment strategy.

Federal student loans come with various repayment options designed to accommodate different financial situations. The Standard Repayment Plan spreads payments over ten years with fixed monthly amounts, which can be challenging but saves money on interest. Income-Driven Repayment Plans (IDRs) adjust your payments based on your income and family size, making them more manageable if your earnings are low. These plans, such as Income-Based Repayment (IBR) or Pay As You Earn (PAYE), can extend the repayment period to 20 or 25 years, but any remaining balance may be forgiven at the end. Public Service Loan Forgiveness (PSLF) is another option for those working in qualifying public service jobs. After making 120 qualifying payments, the remaining loan balance is forgiven, offering significant relief for those in public service careers.

Refinancing and consolidating loans are strategies that can simplify payments and reduce interest rates. Refinancing involves taking out a new loan with a lower interest rate to pay off existing loans, which can save you money over time. However, refinancing federal loans with a private lender means losing access to federal repayment plans and forgiveness programs, which is a significant drawback. Consolidating federal loans through a Direct Consolidation Loan allows you to combine multiple federal loans into a single loan with a fixed interest rate. This can simplify your payments but may result in a slightly higher interest rate. Weighing the pros and cons of each option is essential to determine the best strategy for your situation.

Balancing student loan payments with other financial goals can be challenging, but not impossible. Don't forget to include your student loans in the debt calculator or app that you are using so it gets included in your debt summary and can be included in your debt repayments each month. Creating a budget that includes your loan payments is crucial. Start by listing your income and all expenses, including your student loan payments, which we covered in Chapter 2. Managing student loans while saving for other goals requires careful planning and discipline. Remember, every small step you take towards managing your student loans and saving for the future brings you closer to financial stability and peace of mind.

CHAPTER 3

3.6 Avoiding Common Debt Traps

Navigating the financial landscape can be tricky, and it's easy to fall into common debt traps. Payday loans are one such trap that can quickly become a financial nightmare. These loans offer quick cash but come with exorbitant interest rates, sometimes exceeding 400% APR. They create a cycle of debt that's hard to escape. Families often turn to payday loans in moments of desperation, thinking they'll be a short-term fix, only to find themselves trapped by the high costs and inability to repay on time. Try to avoid these loans if at all possible.

Rent-to-own agreements are another pitfall. While they may seem like an attractive option for acquiring furniture or electronics without a credit check, they end up costing much more in the long run. The convenience of small weekly payments hides the reality that you'll pay significantly more than the item's retail price by the end of the agreement. These arrangements exploit families who may not have the cash upfront or access to traditional credit, locking them into costly contracts.

Buy now, pay later credit options have become increasingly popular, especially for online shopping. While spreading payments over several months can ease immediate financial strain, the high monthly fees and the potential for missed payments (including penalty fees) can lead to financial trouble. These plans often don't require a credit check, making them accessible but risky. If you miss a payment, the fees can quickly add up, turning a seemingly manageable purchase into a financial burden.

Emotions and behaviors play a significant role in falling into these debt traps. Stress and desperation can cloud judgment, leading to poor financial decisions. When you're worried about making ends meet, the temptation of quick cash from a payday loan or the allure of rent-to-own agreements can be hard to resist. Financial anxiety can make you feel cornered, pushing you toward options that seem like immediate solutions but are detrimental in the long run.

To avoid these traps, consider seeking financial counseling or advice before taking on new debt. Financial counselors can provide objective guidance, helping you explore all your options and understand the long-term implications of your choices. Community resources and assistance programs can offer support without the high costs associated with payday loans or rent-to-own agreements. If you're struggling to afford necessities, look into local food banks, utility assistance programs, or housing aid. These resources can provide temporary relief, giving you time to find more sustainable solutions.

One of the simplest yet most effective strategies for avoiding debt traps is to adopt the mindset: <u>if you don't have the money, don't buy it</u>. This approach requires discipline but can save you from the cycle of debt. Do not go into debt for a new wardrobe or discretionary spending like a new bike or kitchen appliances. This is careless spending and should only be spent when you have paid down your debt. Save for large purchases instead of relying on high-cost credit options. Building an emergency fund can also provide a buffer, reducing the temptation to turn to payday loans or buy now, pay later schemes when unexpected expenses arise.

Real-life examples can provide inspiration and practical insights. Take the case of the Thompson family, who found themselves caught in a payday loan cycle. They sought help from a financial counselor who helped them create a budget, prioritize their debts, and find alternative resources. Over time, they paid off their payday loans and started building savings. Similarly, the Horton family avoided the trap of rent-to-own agreements by saving for their purchases. They used a combination of budgeting and community resources to meet their needs without falling into costly contracts.

Avoiding common debt traps involves recognizing the pitfalls, understanding the psychological factors at play, and implementing practical strategies to steer clear. Seeking financial counseling, exploring community resources, and adopting a disciplined approach to spending can help you avoid high-cost credit options that lead to long-term financial trouble. By learning from the experiences of others, you can navigate the financial landscape more wisely and build a secure future for your family. Ideally, from the advice in this book and other people around you, you can upskill and educate yourself so you can make better financial decisions moving forward and create a compelling financial future.

Navigating the world of debt can be challenging, but understanding different types of debt, effective repayment strategies, and how to avoid common traps can make a significant difference. After finishing this chapter, you should have a solid game plan to pay down your debt, with a hard end date of when it will be paid. In the meantime, minimize your expenses and concentrate on paying down your debt as fast as possible.

Don't move on to the next chapter without doing the following;

1. Choose one of the apps, Undebt.it and Debt Payoff Planner, or go old school and do a spreadsheet or write on paper, and list your debts. List the balance, APR, and minimum monthly payment
2. From Chapter 2, understand how much you can commit to paying off your debt without putting yourself under financial pressure. Sacrifices like canceling a streaming service can help you pay down the debt faster or additional income
3. Pay down your debt every month and keep track of it in the app you decide to use
4. Often they have a graphical representation of how much you owe and the date you will pay it down. Print this out and stick it on the fridge, so the whole family can see and get involved in
5. Call your debt providers and ask for a rate reduction
6. Apply for, if possible, a new balance transfer credit card

As we move forward, let's explore how to invest wisely and build a solid financial future for you and your family.

Chapter 4

Investing Basics for Families

Imagine this: You're sitting with your family around the dinner table, and your teenager asks about saving for college. You suddenly realize that beyond your regular savings account, you don't have a clear plan for growing your money. This is a common scenario for many families. Investing can seem intimidating, but it's one of the most effective ways to build long-term wealth and secure your financial future.

4.1 Introduction to Investing: Why It Matters

Investing is crucial for long-term financial growth. Unlike saving, where your money sits in a bank account earning minimal interest, investing allows your money to grow at a much faster rate. Inflation, which is the gradual increase in prices over time, can erode the purchasing power of your savings. For example, if you save $10,000 today, that money might only be worth $7,000 in terms of purchasing power in 20 years. However, if you invest that same $10,000, it has the potential to grow significantly, outpacing inflation and increasing your wealth.

Consider a real-life scenario: If you had invested $1,000 in a diversified stock portfolio 30 years ago, that investment could be worth over $16,000 today, assuming an average annual return of 10%. This growth is due to the power of compound interest, where your earnings generate even more earnings over time. Investing early allows you to harness this power, significantly increasing your wealth over the decades.

Starting early is one of the best advantages you can give yourself when it comes to investing. The earlier you start, the more time your money has to grow. For instance, if you start investing $200 a month at age 25 with an average annual return of 7%, you could have over $500,000 by the time you're 65. If you wait until you're 40 to start investing the same amount, you'd only have about $120,000 by age 65. Time in the market is a powerful ally, as it allows your investments to grow exponentially.

Charts showing the growth of investments started at different ages can be eye-opening. They clearly illustrate how starting early can lead to significantly larger returns. For example, a chart might show that an investment started at age 25 grows much larger than one started at age 40, even if the monthly contributions are the same. This visual representation can be a powerful motivator to start investing as soon as possible.

Many people avoid investing because they believe it's too risky or complicated. However, investing doesn't have to be either. One common misconception is that investing is akin to gambling. While gambling relies on chance, investing relies on research, strategy, and time. Another myth is that you need a lot of money to start investing. In reality, you can begin with small amounts and gradually increase your investments as you become more comfortable. Many investment platforms allow you to start with as little as $50.

It's essential to shift your mindset towards viewing investing as a necessary part of financial planning. Investing is not just an option; it's a crucial step for securing your financial future. Families who invest wisely can achieve financial security, allowing them to afford major life expenses like buying a home, funding education, and enjoying retirement. For example, the Shirley family started investing small amounts each month in their 30s. Over time, their investments grew, enabling them to pay for their children's college education and retire comfortably.

Financial experts often stress the importance of investing. Warren Buffett, one of the most successful investors of all time, famously said, "The stock market is designed to transfer money from the Active to the Patient." This quote highlights the importance of patience and long-term thinking in investing. The power of compound interest, as Albert Einstein called it, is "the eighth wonder of the world." Understanding and utilizing this principle can significantly impact your financial future.

Investing is essential for building long-term wealth and securing your financial future. By starting early, you can take advantage of compound interest and grow your money significantly over time. Don't let common misconceptions hold you back. Investing is accessible and can be done in small amounts. Shifting your mindset to view investing as a necessary step in your financial plan will set you on the path to financial security. Investing should only be done once you have paid down your debt and built up your emergency fund.

4.2 Understanding Stocks, Bonds, and Mutual Funds

When you buy a stock, you're purchasing a small piece of a company, known as a share. Owning a share means you have a stake in the company's future profits and losses. Think of it as owning a tiny slice of the business. If the company does well, the value of your shares can increase, and you might receive dividends—payments made to shareholders from the company's profits. For example, consider well-known companies like Apple or Amazon. If you had bought shares in these companies a decade ago, your investment could have grown significantly due to their strong performance over the years. Stocks can be a powerful way to grow your wealth, but they do come with risks, as the value can fluctuate based on the company's performance and market conditions.

Bonds, on the other hand, are essentially loans you give to a company or government in exchange for regular interest payments. When you buy a bond, you're lending money to the issuer for a set period. In return, the issuer pays you interest, typically twice a year, and returns the principal amount at the end of the bond's term. Government bonds are considered safer because they're backed by the government. U.S. Treasury bonds, for instance, are seen as very low-risk investments. Corporate bonds are issued by companies and usually offer higher interest rates but come with more risk. Bonds generate income through these interest payments, making them a more stable but lower-return investment compared to stocks.

Mutual funds pool money from multiple investors to buy a diversified portfolio of stocks, bonds, or other securities. This pooling allows investors to own a small piece of many different investments, reducing risk through diversification. Instead of putting all your eggs in one basket, mutual funds spread your money across various assets. This diversification can help mitigate the impact of poor performance by any single investment. Popular mutual funds, like the Vanguard 500 Index Fund, track the performance of the S&P 500, providing exposure to 500 of the largest U.S. companies. These funds have a track record of stable returns over the long term, making them a popular choice for many investors to start their investing.

Each of these investment vehicles—stocks, bonds, and mutual funds—has different risk and return profiles. Stocks generally offer higher potential returns but come with higher risk. They are suitable for investors with a longer time horizon who can weather market ups and downs. It does require you to do some research on the company to see if it's a good stock to buy. Bonds, while offering lower returns, provide more stability and regular income, making them ideal for conservative investors or those nearing retirement. Mutual funds offer a balance between the two by providing diversification, which can reduce risk while still offering a reasonable return. They are a good option for those who prefer a more hands-off investment approach, as they are managed by professional fund managers.

Choosing the right mix of these investments depends on your financial goals, risk tolerance, and investment horizon. For example, a young family saving for college might prioritize stocks for their higher growth potential.

In contrast, a family nearing retirement might lean more towards bonds for stability and income. Mutual funds can serve as a core component of any portfolio, offering a diversified investment that aligns with various financial goals. Understanding these options helps you make informed decisions, ensuring your investments support your long-term financial objectives and your age when starting.

4.3 The Power of Compound Interest

Compound interest is one of the most powerful concepts in investing. It's the interest calculated on both the initial principal and the accumulated interest from previous periods. Unlike simple interest, which is only calculated on the principal, compound interest grows your money at an accelerated rate. Imagine you invest $1,000 at an annual interest rate of 5%. With simple interest, you'd earn $50 each year. But with compound interest, you'd earn $50 in the first year, and then interest on $1,050 in the second year, resulting in $52.50, and so on. Over time, this compounding effect can lead to exponential growth, far outpacing simple interest.

Understanding why compound interest is crucial for long-term investing is key to building wealth. Let's compare two scenarios: one where you invest $10,000 with simple interest and another with compound interest. With simple interest at 5%, your investment grows to $15,000 over 10 years. This assumes you withdraw the interest earned every year. However, with compound interest at the same rate, your investment grows to approximately $16,470. Charts can help visualize this growth. A chart comparing investments with and without compound interest clearly shows the exponential curve of compounded investments. Real-life examples further illustrate this; consider someone who started investing $200 a month at age 25. By age 65, with an average annual return of 7%, their investments could grow to over $500,000, thanks to compound interest.

Practical examples make the concept of compound interest more relatable.

The Rule of 72 is a simple way to estimate how long it will take for your investment to double. By dividing 72 by your annual rate of return, you get the number of years it will take. For example, with an annual return of 6%, it would take roughly 12 years for your investment to double (72/6=12). Calculations showing the future value of regular investments can also be enlightening. If you invest $100 monthly at a 7% annual return, you will have about $120,000 after 30 years. These calculations highlight the importance of regular, consistent investing.

Starting early is crucial to maximizing the benefits of compound interest. The longer your money has to grow, the more dramatic the compounding effect. Case studies show stark differences between early and late investors. Take Emma and Tom, for instance. Emma starts investing $200 a month at age 25, while Tom starts at 40. Both aim to retire at 65. Emma ends up with over $500,000, while Tom has around $120,000. This difference underscores the importance of time in building wealth. But don't despair if you haven't started investing early, it is better late than never. Parents can also teach their children about compound interest early on. Encourage them to save a portion of their allowance or gift money. Show them how their savings can grow over time with simple charts and calculators. This early education can set them on a path to financial success.

4.4 Diversifying Your Investment Portfolio

Think about your investments like a balanced diet. Just as you wouldn't eat only one type of food for every meal, you shouldn't put all your money into one type of investment. Diversification is the practice of spreading your investments across different assets to reduce risk. Imagine having a portfolio that is entirely made up of stocks during a market downturn. The value of your portfolio could plummet, causing significant financial stress. However, if your portfolio includes a mix of stocks, bonds, real estate, and other assets, the decline in one area might be offset by stability or gains in another. Diversified portfolios tend to be more resilient during market fluctuations, providing a safety net that helps you weather financial storms.

When diversifying your portfolio, it's essential to include a variety of asset types. Stocks, with their potential for high returns, are a common choice. Bonds, which offer more stability and regular income, balance out the riskier stocks. Including international investments can further diversify your portfolio. These investments give you exposure to different economies and markets, reducing your reliance on the performance of your home country's economy. For example, while the U.S. market might be down, the European or Asian markets might be performing well, helping to balance your overall portfolio. All this means is potentially buying stocks and mutual funds on other stock markets across the world, like in London, Hong Kong, or Australia. Until you're a little more experienced maybe leave this initially and concentrate on the US stock market.

Balancing risk and return through diversification involves creating a portfolio that matches your risk tolerance. Everyone has a different comfort level with risk, and it's crucial to understand yours. Risk assessment tools and questionnaires can help you determine your risk tolerance. These tools ask questions about your financial goals, investment timeframe, and how you react to market volatility. Based on your answers, they provide insights into the types of investments that might suit you best. Vanguard has a good one on their website under resources and education called an investor questionnaire. For instance, if you have a low-risk tolerance, you might focus more on bonds and less on stocks. Conversely, if you're comfortable with higher risk, a larger portion of your portfolio might be in stocks.

Maintaining a diversified portfolio requires ongoing management. Regularly rebalancing your portfolio ensures that it remains aligned with your risk tolerance and financial goals. Over time, some investments might grow faster than others, causing your portfolio to become unbalanced. For example, if your stocks perform exceptionally well, they might take up a larger percentage of your portfolio than you initially intended. Rebalancing involves selling some of the overperforming assets and buying more of the underperforming ones to restore your desired asset allocation. This process might seem counterintuitive, but it helps maintain the risk level you're comfortable with. Or it might mean when you invest additional money, you might put it into a more conservative investment to balance it out that way.

Let's use a practical example. When you first invest, you have $10,000 to invest. You invest $6,000 into shares in Amazon, $2,000 into government bonds, and $2,000 into a mutual fund. This is a risk profile you are comfortable with at 60% stocks, 20% bonds, and 20% mutual funds. The last 5 years' performance for Amazon has seen share price grow by 105%, government bonds have grown by 3.65% and the Vanguard mutual fund has grown by 10%. So the initial $10,000 which was allocated into $6,000 into shares in Amazon, $2,000 into government bonds, and $2,000 into a mutual fund in 5 years is now $12,300 in Amazon shares, $2,392 in government bonds, and $3,221 in mutual funds. So your portfolio has grown from $10,000 to $17,913 - good job! But now your shares have grown from 60% of your portfolio ($6,000 divided by $10,000) to 69% (12,300 divided by $17,913), government bonds from 20% down to 13%, and mutual funds from 20% to 18%. Do you sell down some of your Amazon shares and buy more government bonds? They have performed well for you, but by doing this you do bank the upside you have already received and none of the downside. If you do sell some of these shares, it is a taxable event, so you will have to pay tax on the upside profit. Another option could be that if you add more money into your investment portfolio, as I am going to show you below, you might choose to buy more government bonds and this will help rebalance your portfolio without selling any Amazon shares.

Using low-cost index funds for diversification is a practical approach. Index funds track the performance of a market index, like the S&P 500, offering broad market exposure at a low cost. They provide instant diversification because they include a wide range of assets within a single fund. For example, by investing in an S&P 500 index fund, you get exposure to 500 of the largest companies in the U.S., reducing the risk associated with any single company's performance. The low expense ratios of index funds mean that more of your money stays invested, compounding over time to grow your wealth.

Diversifying your investment portfolio is about spreading your investments across different assets to reduce risk and increase potential returns. Including a mix of stocks, bonds, real estate, commodities, and international investments creates a balanced portfolio that can withstand market fluctuations. Regular rebalancing ensures your portfolio stays aligned with your goals, and using low-cost index funds provides an easy way to achieve broad diversification.

4.5 Investing in Low-Cost Index Funds

Let's talk about index funds. These are types of mutual funds designed to mimic the performance of a market index, such as the S&P 500. When you invest in an index fund, your money is spread across all the companies in the index. This diversification helps reduce risk. Unlike actively managed funds, where a manager picks stocks in an attempt to beat the market, index funds simply aim to match market performance. This means they require less management, and thus, have lower fees. Actively managed funds often involve higher costs due to the need for research and management, but they don't always outperform the market.

Low-cost index funds are a great choice for beginner investors. One of their main benefits is lower fees compared to actively managed funds. These fees, known as expense ratios, can eat into your returns over time. For instance, an actively managed fund might charge 1% annually, while an index fund could charge as little as 0.03%. Over decades, these savings can add up significantly. Historical data supports this: index funds have consistently outperformed many actively managed funds over the long term. The lower fees and broad market exposure make them an attractive option for those new to investing.

When selecting the right index funds, consider several factors. Expense ratios are crucial because lower fees mean more of your money stays invested, compounding over time. Tracking error, which measures how closely the fund follows its index, is another important factor. You want a fund with minimal tracking error to ensure it accurately reflects the index's performance. Fund size also matters; larger funds tend to be more stable and have lower expense ratios. Examples of popular index funds include the Vanguard 500 Index Fund, which tracks the S&P 500, and the Fidelity Total Market Index Fund. Both offer low fees and broad market exposure, making them solid choices for any portfolio.

Getting started with index funds involves a few simple steps. First, open an account with a brokerage like Charles Schwab or Vanguard. These platforms offer a range of index funds and have user-friendly interfaces. Once your account is set up, decide how much you want to invest initially and set up automatic investments. This means a set amount of money will be transferred from your bank account to your investment account regularly, ensuring consistent contributions without having to remember each month. Monitoring and adjusting your portfolio as needed is also important. Periodically review your investments to ensure they align with your goals and risk tolerance. If your financial situation changes, you might need to adjust your investment strategy.

Index funds can also serve as a gateway to other investments like shares and bonds. Most brokerage platforms that offer index funds will also allow you to invest in individual stocks and bonds. This integration makes it easy to manage all your investments in one place. For instance, you might start with a low-cost index fund and gradually diversify by adding individual stocks or bonds as you become more comfortable with investing. This approach offers a balanced mix of growth and stability, helping you build a robust financial portfolio over time.

4.6 Setting Up a Family Investment Plan

Having a family investment plan is like setting a roadmap for your financial future. It ensures that everyone in the family is on the same page and working toward common financial goals. A clear plan helps you align your investment strategies with your long-term objectives, whether it's buying a home, funding your children's education, or planning for retirement. For instance, the Curry family created an investment plan focusing on saving for their kids' college education. They allocated funds into a low-cost index fund to ensure they met their goals without compromising their everyday needs. Each family's plan will look different based on their unique objectives, but the foundation remains the same—aligning investments with long-term goals.

Determining your investment objectives and risk tolerance is the next critical step. Start by clearly defining what you aim to achieve with your investments. Are you looking to save for a down payment on a house within five years, or are you planning for retirement in 30 years? Your goals will determine your investment strategy. Tools like investment goal-setting worksheets can help you outline these objectives, as we did in Chapter 1. Similarly, understanding your risk tolerance is essential. Some people can handle market volatility, while others prefer more stable investments. Risk tolerance questionnaires can guide you in assessing your comfort level with risk, helping you choose appropriate investments that align with your financial goals and emotional comfort.

Creating a family investment plan involves several steps but don't worry, it's manageable. Start by identifying your investment goals and time horizons. Break down your goals into short-term, medium-term, and long-term categories. This will help you select the right investment vehicles for each goal. For example, short-term goals might be best served by bonds or high-yield savings accounts, while long-term goals could benefit from stocks or mutual funds. Next, assign roles and responsibilities within the family. Maybe one person tracks the investments, another handles the budget, and a third person keeps everyone updated on progress. This collaborative approach ensures that everyone is involved and committed to the plan's success.

Regular review and adjustment of your investment plan are crucial for ongoing success. Family circumstances and market conditions can change, and your investment plan needs to adapt accordingly. Set up regular family Money meetings to review the investment plan. These meetings should be monthly to start with but as you become more stable they can move to quarterly, whatever works best for you and your family. During these sessions, discuss any changes in income, expenses, or financial goals. Adjust the plan as needed to ensure it remains aligned with your objectives. For instance, if you receive a windfall, you might decide to increase your investment contributions or pay down debt faster. Conversely, if you face an unexpected expense, you might need to adjust your savings rate temporarily. This ongoing management ensures that your plan remains relevant and effective.

In summary, having a family investment plan helps you achieve your financial goals by aligning your investment strategies with long-term objectives. Use tools like goal-setting worksheets and risk tolerance questionnaires to determine your investment objectives and comfort with risk. Follow a step-by-step process to create a detailed plan, assigning roles and responsibilities to ensure everyone is involved. Regularly review and adjust the plan to keep it on track, adapting to changes in family circumstances and market conditions. This proactive approach not only secures your financial future but also fosters a sense of teamwork and shared responsibility within the family.

Don't move on to the next chapter without doing the following;

1. Open a brokerage account with either Charles Schwab or Vanguard
2. Google best-performing index funds. Check their expense ratios and returns over 5 years
3. Pick one and buy one. Congratulations, you are an investor
4. Set up an automatic payment or use the money from round-up budgeting apps in Chapter 2 like Raiz to keep buying each month
5. Track your portfolio and report progress in your monthly Money nights

As we move forward, let's explore the next chapter on retirement planning essentials, where we'll discuss how to ensure a comfortable and financially secure retirement.

Chapter 5

Retirement Planning Essentials

Imagine it's a typical Saturday morning, and you're sipping coffee while scrolling through social media. You stumble upon a post from an old friend who just retired and is now traveling the world. You feel a pang of envy and a bit of anxiety. How did they manage to retire comfortably while you're still trying to figure out how to save enough? This scenario is common, and it highlights the importance of planning for retirement. Understanding how much money you'll need and how to save for it can make all the difference in achieving the retirement of your dreams.

5.1 Calculating Your Retirement Needs

Accurately calculating your retirement needs is crucial. Without a clear understanding of how much money you will need, you risk underestimating your expenses, which can lead to financial stress in your golden years. Underestimating your retirement needs can have a significant impact. Imagine reaching retirement age only to realize you don't have enough savings to cover your basic expenses. This could mean having to downsize your home, cut back on leisure activities, or even return to work. Longevity and rising healthcare costs also play a significant role in retirement planning. People are living longer than ever before, and while this is a blessing, it also means you'll need more money to cover additional years of living expenses. Healthcare costs tend to rise as we age, and without proper planning, these expenses can quickly deplete your savings.

To estimate your annual retirement expenses, start with the basics. Consider your housing costs. Will you own your home outright, or will you still have a mortgage? Don't forget to account for property taxes, maintenance, and utilities. Next, think about healthcare costs. Even with Medicare, you'll likely have out-of-pocket expenses, including premiums, co-pays, and prescription drugs. Travel and leisure are also important. Retirement is a time to enjoy life, so include the cost of vacations, hobbies, and entertainment. Finally, adjust for inflation. Prices for goods and services will continue to rise, so it's essential to factor this into your calculations. A good rule of thumb is to estimate an annual inflation rate of 2-3%.

Several tools and calculators can help you estimate your retirement needs accurately. Online retirement calculators from reputable financial institutions like Vanguard and NerdWallet are excellent resources. These calculators allow you to input your current savings, expected expenses, and other variables to give you a personalized estimate of how much you'll need to save. For a more detailed approach, consider using the Retirement Needs Worksheet from Charles Schwab. This worksheet helps you break down your expenses and adjust for inflation, providing a comprehensive view of your retirement needs.

Social Security will also play a role in your retirement planning. It's essential to understand how much you can expect to receive from Social Security based on your earnings history. You can estimate your benefits by visiting the Social Security Administration's website and using their online calculator. The age at which you claim benefits can significantly impact the amount you receive. For example, claiming benefits at 62, the earliest age you can start will result in a reduced monthly benefit compared to waiting until your full retirement age, which is typically around 66 or 67. Delaying benefits even further, up to age 70, can increase your monthly payments substantially. Understanding these nuances can help you make an informed decision about when to start receiving Social Security benefits.

By taking the time to accurately calculate your retirement needs, you can ensure you're on track for a comfortable and secure retirement, and if you're not, adjust accordingly. Consider all potential expenses, adjust for inflation, and utilize reliable tools and calculators. Don't forget to factor in Social Security and make informed decisions about when to claim your benefits. With careful planning, you can look forward to enjoying your golden years without financial worry.

5.2 Understanding Different Retirement Accounts

When planning for retirement, choosing the right accounts can make a significant difference in how much you save and grow your wealth. Let's start by defining some common retirement savings vehicles. A 401(k) is an employer-sponsored retirement plan that allows employees to contribute a portion of their salary, often with matching contributions from the employer. These plans offer tax-deferred growth, meaning you won't pay taxes on your contributions or earnings until you withdraw the money in retirement. Similarly, a 403(b) plan is available to employees of public schools and certain non-profit organizations, offering the same tax-deferred benefits as a 401(k).

Individual Retirement Accounts (IRAs) are another popular option, and they come in several forms. A Traditional IRA allows you to contribute pre-tax dollars, which can reduce your taxable income for the year. The money grows tax-deferred, and you pay taxes when you withdraw it in retirement. In contrast, a Roth IRA involves contributions made with after-tax dollars. While you don't get an immediate tax break, your money grows tax-free, and qualified withdrawals are also tax-free. SEP IRAs are designed for self-employed individuals and small business owners, offering higher contribution limits than Traditional and Roth IRAs. These plans allow employers to make contributions to their employees' retirement savings, providing a flexible and tax-advantaged way to save.

The differences between employer-sponsored accounts like 401(k)s and individual accounts like IRAs are significant. Employer-sponsored accounts often come with the added benefit of employer matching contributions, essentially free money added to your retirement savings. For example, if your employer matches 50% of your contributions up to 6% of your salary, contributing at least that amount maximizes your benefits. Individual accounts, on the other hand, offer more flexibility in terms of investment choices and control but lack the employer match.

Tax advantages and implications vary between account types. Traditional IRAs and 401(k)s offer tax-deferred growth, which means you won't pay taxes on your contributions or earnings until you withdraw the money in retirement. This can be a significant advantage if you expect to be in a lower tax bracket when you retire. On the other hand, Roth IRAs provide tax-free growth and tax-free withdrawals, making them an excellent choice if you expect to be in a higher tax bracket in retirement. With Roth IRAs, you pay taxes upfront, but your withdrawals are tax-free, which can be beneficial if you anticipate higher tax rates in the future. The best option here is to speak to a financial advisor as the options change so regularly and they know all the tax benefits too.

Understanding contribution limits and rules for each account is crucial to maximizing your retirement savings. For 2023, the annual contribution limit for 401(k) plans is $22,500, with an additional catch-up contribution of $7,500 for individuals aged 50 and older. Traditional and Roth IRAs have a combined annual contribution limit of $6,500, with a $1,000 catch-up contribution for those aged 50 and older. SEP IRAs allow contributions of up to 25% of your compensation or $66,000, whichever is less. These limits are essential to keep in mind as you plan your contributions to ensure you're taking full advantage of tax-advantaged savings opportunities.

Choosing the right retirement accounts depends on several factors, including your current and future tax brackets and whether your employer offers matching contributions. If you're in a higher tax bracket now but expect to be in a lower bracket in retirement, contributing to a Traditional IRA or 401(k) might be more beneficial due to the immediate tax break. Conversely, if you anticipate being in a higher tax bracket in retirement, a Roth IRA's tax-free withdrawals could be more advantageous. Employer matching contributions are another critical consideration. If your employer offers a match, it's wise to contribute enough to take full advantage of this benefit, as it essentially provides free money you wouldn't otherwise get. Check you can afford this in your budgeting app cash flow in Chapter 2.

Consider different scenarios when selecting the best account for your situation. For example, if you're a young professional with many years until retirement, a Roth IRA might be a good choice due to the potential for tax-free growth over a long period. If you're a small business owner, a SEP IRA offers higher contribution limits, allowing you to save more aggressively. Each individual's circumstances will vary, so it's essential to evaluate your specific needs and goals when choosing retirement accounts.

5.3 Strategies for Long-Term Retirement Savings

One of the most powerful concepts in retirement savings is compounding. Compounding can significantly grow your retirement funds over time by earning interest not just on your initial investment, but also on the accumulated interest from previous periods. Imagine planting a tree. Initially, it starts small, but as it grows, it produces more leaves and branches, which in turn generate even more growth. The earlier you start saving, the more time your money has to compound, resulting in exponential growth. For instance, if you start saving $200 a month at age 25 with an annual return of 7%, you could end up with over $500,000 by age 65. However, if you start at 40, you might only have around $120,000 by the same age. The difference is striking and underscores the importance of starting early.

Automatic contributions are a game-changer when it comes to building your retirement savings consistently. Setting up automatic contributions through payroll deduction ensures that a portion of your salary goes directly into your retirement account before you even see it. This "set it and forget it" method removes the temptation to spend the money elsewhere and makes saving a seamless part of your financial routine. Many employers offer the option to set up automatic contributions to your 401(k) or similar plans, making it easy to stay on track. If you have an IRA, you can use apps or bank features to automate contributions, ensuring that you regularly add to your savings without having to remember to make manual transfers.

Maximizing employer-sponsored plans is another crucial strategy for long-term retirement savings. If your employer offers a 401(k) plan with matching contributions, it's essential to contribute enough to receive the full match. This is essentially free money added to your retirement savings. For example, if your employer matches 50% of your contributions up to 6% of your salary, not contributing at least 6% means leaving money on the table. Understanding vesting schedules is also important. Vesting refers to the length of time you must work for an employer before you fully own the employer's contributions to your retirement plan. If you leave the company before you're fully vested, you might forfeit some or all of those contributions. Knowing your vesting schedule helps you make informed decisions about your employment and retirement planning. Ask your employer's personnel department about these when you catch up with them.

Diversification within your retirement accounts is crucial for managing risk and ensuring steady growth. By spreading your investments across various asset classes, you can protect your portfolio from significant losses if one sector under-performs. Allocating funds to stocks, bonds, and other assets provides a balanced approach that can weather market fluctuations. For instance, stocks typically offer higher returns but come with more risk, while bonds provide stability and regular income. Regularly rebalancing your portfolio helps maintain your desired allocation. This means periodically reviewing your investments and making adjustments to ensure that your portfolio remains diversified according to your risk tolerance and financial goals. For example, if stocks have performed well and now make up a larger portion of your portfolio than intended, you might sell some stocks and buy bonds to bring your allocation back in line or change your investment options. When you first open your retirement account, your employer will normally suggest which brokerage or bank it is done through. They will then send you paperwork where you get to choose your investment strategy. You can choose to be aggressive, with a higher performing fund, or conservative, with a lower return and it will give you a history of how each option has performed over time. Again, you can get help with this or look at the results yourself based on your age and your outcome and make a choice. Don't think because you choose one option now doesn't mean you can't change your investment options later. I log on to my brokerage account each quarter to see how it's performing, if I'm happy with the returns, I log off; otherwise, you can check the other funds' performance and you can make the change right there online. Make sure you check the performance of your retirement account, as steps you make today have an impact on your balance in the future. Review the performance when you have you Money night meetings.

Incorporating these strategies into your retirement planning can significantly impact your financial future. Compounding allows your investments to grow exponentially over time, making it crucial to start saving early. Automatic contributions ensure consistent savings, removing the need for manual transfers and reducing the temptation to spend. Maximizing employer-sponsored plans, particularly by taking full advantage of matching contributions and understanding vesting schedules, adds to your retirement savings. Diversification within your retirement accounts spreads risk and offers a balanced approach to growth. By rebalancing your portfolio periodically, you can maintain your desired allocation and protect your investments from market volatility. These strategies collectively pave the way for a secure and comfortable retirement, allowing you to enjoy your golden years with peace of mind.

5.4 Balancing Retirement Savings with Other Financial Goals

Balancing multiple financial priorities can feel like juggling flaming torches while riding a unicycle. Saving for retirement is just one piece of the puzzle. Many families also need to save for their children's education, buy a home, and pay off debt—all while managing day-to-day expenses. Each of these goals is important, and finding a way to prioritize them can be challenging. For instance, you might wonder whether it's better to put extra money towards your mortgage or into your retirement fund. Or maybe you're torn between saving for your child's college education and paying off high-interest debt. These competing priorities can make financial planning feel overwhelming.

To help prioritize your financial goals, start by using a goal-setting worksheet like we did in Chapter 1. This tool can help you rank your goals based on their importance and urgency. For example, immediate needs like paying off high-interest debt might take precedence over long-term goals like buying a vacation home. Once you have a clear list, allocate resources accordingly. Financial planning tools, like online calculators and budgeting apps like Empower, can help you visualize the long-term impact of different savings strategies. These tools can show you how much you need to save each month to reach your goals, helping you make informed decisions about where to allocate your money.

Integrated planning is key to achieving multiple financial objectives. By creating a comprehensive financial plan that includes all your major goals, you can see how they fit together and adjust your strategy as needed. For example, if you receive a bonus at work, you might decide to split it between your retirement fund and a college savings account, if you are already debt free. Adjusting contributions to different accounts based on life changes, like a promotion or a new baby, can help you stay on track. This flexible approach ensures that you're making progress on all your goals without neglecting any single one.

Real-life examples can be incredibly inspiring and provide practical insights. Take the Lynett family, for instance. They managed to save for their retirement while also funding their children's college education. They started by creating a detailed financial plan that prioritized paying off high-interest debt first. Once their debt was paid off, they used the amount they were paying down debt to set up automatic contributions to both their retirement accounts and college savings plans. By sticking to their plan and making adjustments as needed, they were able to achieve both goals. Similarly, the Wheaton family found a balance between saving for a down payment on a home and their retirement fund. They used a goal-setting worksheet to rank their priorities and allocate resources accordingly. By keeping a close eye on their budget and making small sacrifices, like cutting back on dining out, they were able to save for both goals simultaneously.

5.5 Avoiding Common Retirement Planning Mistakes

Retirement planning is a critical part of ensuring a comfortable future, but it's easy to make mistakes along the way. One of the most common errors is underestimating retirement expenses. Many people assume they'll spend less in retirement than they do while working, but this isn't always the case. Your spending patterns may change, but new expenses can arise. For example, you might travel more, take up new hobbies, or face unexpected healthcare costs. Failing to account for these potential expenses can leave you under-prepared. Inflation is another factor that often gets overlooked. Even a modest annual inflation rate of 2-3% can significantly erode your purchasing power over time. If you don't adjust your savings plan to account for inflation, you may find that your nest egg doesn't stretch as far as you thought it would.

Another pitfall to avoid is making early withdrawals from your retirement accounts. While it might be tempting to dip into your retirement savings for a big purchase or unexpected expense, doing so can have serious consequences. Early withdrawals often come with hefty tax penalties. For example, if you withdraw funds from a Traditional IRA or 401(k) before age $59\frac{1}{2}$, you may face a 10% penalty on top of regular income taxes. This can significantly reduce your savings. Moreover, taking money out early disrupts the growth potential of your retirement funds. The money you withdraw is no longer compounding, which can have a long-term impact on your overall savings. Think of it like cutting down a tree that's just starting to bear fruit; you're not just losing the immediate benefit but also the future yield.

Emotional investment decisions can also derail your retirement planning.

CHAPTER 5

During market downturns, it's natural to feel anxious and consider selling off investments to avoid further losses. However, panic selling can lock in losses and prevent you from benefiting from the market's eventual recovery. Staying disciplined with your investment strategy is crucial. Stick to your long-term plan, even when the market is volatile. Remember that investing is a marathon, not a sprint. Avoid making decisions based on short-term market movements. Instead, focus on your long-term goals and the overall performance of your portfolio. This disciplined approach can help you navigate market fluctuations without jeopardizing your retirement savings.

Keeping your retirement plans updated is another important aspect of successful retirement planning. Life is full of changes, and your retirement strategy should reflect that. Setting up annual financial check-ups can help you stay on track. During these reviews, take a close look at your income, expenses, and goals. Adjust your retirement contributions if your income has changed or if you have new financial priorities. For example, if you've received a raise, consider increasing your contributions to take advantage of the extra income if your debt is paid off and it aligns with your financial goals. Similarly, if your expenses have increased, you might need to adjust your budget to ensure you're still saving enough for retirement. Regularly updating your plan ensures that it remains relevant and effective, helping you stay on course to achieve your retirement goals. If you feel like you can do this yourself then great, but if you feel like you need a financial advisor's help then you should reach out to one. Ask friends fro recommendations or look one up on Ramsey Solutions website how have Smartvestor Pros across the country. You want these professionals to be smarter than you so you can keep learning. These consultations will cost you, but it should only be a one off fee and you might need one every few years or only as a one off.

These steps can help you avoid common retirement planning mistakes and ensure a more secure financial future. By accurately estimating your expenses, avoiding early withdrawals, staying disciplined with your investments, and keeping your plans updated, you can navigate the complexities of retirement planning with confidence.

5.6 Ensuring a Comfortable Retirement Lifestyle

Planning your retirement lifestyle goes beyond just having enough money to cover the basics. It's about envisioning the life you want to lead and understanding how your activities and hobbies will impact your financial needs. Picture yourself traveling, taking up new hobbies, or finally having the time to volunteer for causes you care about. Each of these activities comes with its own set of costs. Estimating these expenses helps ensure you have the funds to enjoy your retirement to the fullest. For instance, if you plan to travel frequently, you'll need to budget for airfare, accommodations, and other related expenses. Similarly, new hobbies like golfing or crafts can add to your monthly expenditures. Take the time to list out these potential costs to create a realistic budget that aligns with your dream retirement lifestyle.

Maintaining your health and wellness in retirement is crucial, both for your quality of life and your finances. Staying healthy can reduce medical expenses and improve your overall well-being. Budgeting for healthcare and wellness expenses is an essential part of retirement planning. This includes not only routine medical check-ups and treatments but also preventive care and wellness activities. Regular exercise, for example, can help keep you fit and reduce the risk of chronic conditions. Consider joining a gym, taking yoga classes, or even participating in community sports leagues. Preventive healthcare measures, such as vaccinations and screenings, can catch potential health issues early, saving you money and stress in the long run. Allocating funds for these activities ensures that you can maintain a healthy lifestyle without financial strain.

Social connections and community involvement play a significant role in enhancing your retirement experience. Staying socially active can boost your mental and emotional well-being, making your retirement years more fulfilling. Participating in community groups and activities is an excellent way to stay engaged and meet new people. Whether it's joining a book club, attending community events, or taking part in local classes, these activities provide opportunities for social interaction and personal growth. Volunteering is another fantastic way to stay active and contribute to your community. It offers a sense of purpose and can be incredibly rewarding. Many retirees find that volunteering not only enriches their lives but also helps them build new friendships and stay connected.

Creating a sustainable retirement income plan is key to ensuring that your savings last throughout your retirement years. One common strategy is the 4% rule, which suggests withdrawing 4% of your retirement savings each year, so it would last around 25 years. This approach provides a steady income while preserving the bulk of your savings. However, flexibility is important. Adjust your withdrawals based on your investment performance and expenses. For instance, in years when your investments perform well, you might withdraw a bit more, while in lean years, you might tighten your belt. It's also wise to have a mix of income sources, such as Social Security, pensions, and investments, to provide stability and reduce the risk of outliving your savings. By managing your withdrawals carefully and adjusting as needed, you can maintain a comfortable lifestyle without depleting your savings prematurely.

As you plan for retirement, consider all aspects of your desired lifestyle. Estimate the costs of travel, hobbies, and leisure activities to ensure you have the funds to enjoy your retirement fully. Prioritize your health and wellness by budgeting for healthcare and preventive measures, and stay socially active through community involvement and volunteering. Create a sustainable retirement income plan by utilizing strategies like the 4% rule and adjusting withdrawals based on investment performance. By addressing these elements, you can look forward to a fulfilling and financially secure retirement.

Don't move on to the next chapter without doing the following;

1. If you haven't already, discuss retirement account options with your spouse, personnel department, and/or a financial advisor
2. Open a retirement account and choose your investment strategy
3. Start contributions to this account, preferably with an employer match
4. Do quarterly check-ins on your retirement savings in your Money night meetings

5. Find a retirement calculator online, like Vanguard's retirement calculator, and estimate how much you'll need in retirement

Savings for your retirement is essential and it doesn't matter when you start but you should start now. The power of compound interest will be your friend here, so if you make contributions now, you can set and forget and let the returns happen. You'll monitor these in your monthly money meetings, but for now, the hard work has been done, congratulations!

* * *

Make a Difference with Your Review

People who give without expecting anything in return live happier lives. So, let's make a difference together!

Would you help someone just like you—curious about Financial Freedom but unsure where to start?

My mission is to make Financial Freedom understandable for everyone.

But to reach more people, I need your help.

Most people choose books based on reviews. So, I'm asking you to help someone else by leaving a review.

It costs nothing and takes less than a minute but could change someone's financial journey and turn around a family's future. Your review could help...

...one more family get out of debt
　...one parent build their emergency fund for their family
　...one child understand money to start their life out better than they started
　...one more person take control of their finances

CHAPTER 5

...one more dream come true

If you love helping others, you're my kind of person. Thank you from the bottom of my heart!

To make a difference, simply scan the QR code below, or click on the link and leave a review:https://amzn.to/4ecGFVe

Emma Maxwell

Chapter 6

Financial Education for Children

Imagine this: you're at the grocery store with your young child. You give them a few dollars and ask them to pick out their favorite fruit. They carefully examine the apples, bananas, and oranges, trying to decide how to spend their money wisely. This simple exercise helps plant the seeds of financial literacy. Teaching kids about money from an early age can set the foundation for a lifetime of smart financial decisions. It's all about making learning fun and appropriate for their age.

6.1 Age-Appropriate Financial Lessons for Kids

Children's understanding of money evolves as they grow. Their cognitive development affects how they grasp financial concepts. For instance, a toddler might not understand the value of money, but they can recognize different coins and bills. Simple games like coin identification can be both fun and educational for toddlers. You can use everyday moments, like playing pretend store or restaurant, to introduce basic commerce concepts. At this age, it's all about familiarizing them with the physical aspects of money.

As kids enter preschool, they start understanding the concept of saving and spending. You can involve them in clipping coupons and looking for products in the store, discussing how to save money. Playing imaginary restaurants can teach them about setting the table, good manners, and making change. These activities make financial lessons tangible and relatable. By the time they reach elementary school, they can handle simple budgeting. Opening a savings account and discussing interest can be exciting milestones.

For kids aged six to eight, financial education can take on new dimensions. Opening a savings account and discussing the concept of interest becomes more relevant. Encourage them to start saving a portion of their allowance or gift money and they can spend the rest. Take them to the store and get them to calculate how much something will cost and how much change they'll get back. These activities help them grasp the idea of saving and use their math skills at the same time.

As kids approach middle school, they become more capable of understanding comparison shopping. Teach them how to read price labels and compare costs and quality. You can also put them in charge of yard sales to learn about setting values and negotiating. These experiences teach them the value of money and the importance of making informed spending decisions. It's a great age to introduce them to the concept of budgeting by discussing wants versus needs. Going over the family budget together can be an eye-opening experience, helping them understand how money is allocated and spent and how much things cost.

During the teenage years, financial education becomes even more critical. Teaching teens about investing can benefit their financial future significantly. Start with simple concepts like stocks, bonds, and mutual funds. Explain how the stock market works and encourage them to research companies they are familiar with. Setting up a custodial account with parental guidance allows them to start investing early. Using investment apps designed for teens can make the process accessible and engaging. Real-life examples and success stories of teen investors can inspire them to take their first steps into the world of investing.

Parents play a crucial role in modeling good financial behavior. Kids learn by observing, so demonstrating responsible financial habits is essential. For instance, involve them in everyday financial decisions like grocery shopping. Show them how to compare prices, use coupons, and stick to a budget. When planning a family vacation, let them see how you save and budget for the trip. These real-life scenarios provide valuable lessons that stick with them. It's not just about telling them what to do but showing them through your actions. When they're ready, involve them in your monthly family money meeting.

Consider the story of the Appleby family. They made it a point to involve their kids in financial discussions from a young age. They opened savings accounts for their children and encouraged them to save a portion of their allowance. As the kids grew older, they were given more responsibilities, like managing their expenses for school projects and outings. Today, both Johnson children are financially responsible adults, managing their finances with confidence and making informed decisions. Their parents' proactive approach to financial education made all the difference.

Another example is the Manning family. They used everyday activities to teach their children about money. From grocery shopping to planning vacations, the kids were involved in budgeting and saving decisions. The parents also introduced them to investing by setting up custodial accounts and letting them choose stocks to invest in. As teenagers, the Manning kids managed their small investment portfolios, learning valuable lessons about the stock market. Today, they are financially savvy young adults, thanks to the hands-on financial education they received at home.

Teaching financial literacy at various developmental stages ensures that kids grasp the concepts appropriate for their age. For toddlers, it's about recognizing coins and playing simple money games. Preschoolers can learn about saving and spending through everyday activities like clipping coupons. Elementary school kids can handle simple budgeting and saving with the help of savings accounts and getting change back from a purchase. Middle schoolers benefit from comparison shopping and understanding wants versus needs. Teenagers can start learning about investing and managing their finances.

Parents play a pivotal role in this process. By modeling good financial behavior and involving kids in everyday financial decisions, you can set a strong foundation for their financial future. Real-life examples and success stories show that these efforts pay off. With the right approach, you can help your children grow into financially responsible adults, ready to navigate the complexities of managing money.

6.2 Fun, Interactive Exercises for Teaching Money Skills

Teaching kids about money doesn't have to be a dry, boring process. Making financial learning fun can be incredibly effective. Think about the last time your child was completely absorbed in a game. That same level of engagement can be harnessed to teach valuable money skills. Games and activities turn abstract financial concepts into tangible experiences, making them easier for kids to grasp. When children play, they learn without even realizing it. This interactive approach keeps them interested and helps the lessons stick.

There are numerous age-appropriate games and activities that can teach various financial concepts. For elementary kids, "The Allowance Game" is a fantastic choice. In this board game, kids earn money by doing chores and navigating spending and saving decisions. It's a fun way to introduce the basics of earning and managing money. For teens, online financial literacy games can be both engaging and educational. Games like "Financial Football" combine the excitement of sports with personal finance questions, making learning competitive and enjoyable. These games cover topics like budgeting, credit, and investing, providing a comprehensive introduction to financial literacy.

Hands-on learning experiences offer another powerful way to reinforce financial lessons. Creating a DIY savings bank can be a fun craft project that also teaches the importance of saving. Grab an empty jar or box, let your child decorate it, and label it as their "savings bank." Encourage them to deposit a portion of their allowance or gift money into the bank regularly. This visual and tactile experience helps them understand the concept of saving and see their progress over time. Another effective activity is role-playing scenarios like running a mock store. Set up a mini-store at home with items and price tags. Give your child some play money and let them shop. This exercise teaches them about pricing, making change, and budgeting their money.

To help you get started, here are some step-by-step instructions for a simple budgeting game. First, gather some play money and a variety of household items with price tags. Divide the play money among the participants. Each person takes turns "shopping" for items, ensuring they stay within their budget. After everyone has made their purchases, discuss their choices. Did they prioritize needs over wants? Did they run out of money? This game makes budgeting a hands-on, practical experience.

Interactive methods like games and activities keep children engaged and make learning about money enjoyable. They turn financial education into a fun experience rather than a chore. Whether it's playing "The Allowance Game," participating in online financial literacy games, or creating a DIY savings bank, these activities offer valuable lessons in a memorable way. Hands-on exercises like running a mock store or a lemonade stand provide practical experiences that reinforce financial concepts. By incorporating these fun, interactive exercises into your routine, you can help your children develop essential money skills that will serve them well throughout their lives.

6.3 Encouraging Savings Habits in Young Children

Teaching children to save from an early age sets the stage for financial success as they grow older. Imagine your child receiving their weekly allowance and immediately spending it all on candy or toys. While this is normal for kids, guiding them to save a portion of their money can cultivate a habit that benefits them throughout their lives. Early savings habits are crucial because they teach children the value of delayed gratification. Instead of spending money as soon as they get it, children learn to set aside funds for future needs or desires. This ability to wait and save can translate into more significant financial successes in adulthood, such as saving for a car, a home, or even retirement.

Making saving fun and rewarding can motivate children to develop this essential habit. One way to do this is by setting up a "savings challenge" with rewards. For example, you could challenge your child to save a certain amount of money over a month. If they reach the goal, they earn a reward, such as a small toy or a special outing. This approach turns saving into a game, making it exciting and engaging. Visual aids like savings charts or jars can also be incredibly effective. Create a savings chart where your child can color in sections as they save money. Alternatively, use a clear jar so they can see their savings grow. These visual cues provide a tangible representation of their progress, making the abstract concept of saving more concrete.

Setting specific, achievable savings goals is vital for encouraging children to save. Help your child set both short-term and long-term goals. Short-term goals might include saving for a new toy or a special treat, while long-term goals could be saving for a bike or a trip to the amusement park. To make goal-setting effective, involve your child in the planning process. Sit down together and discuss what they want to save for and how much it will cost. Break down the total amount into smaller, manageable chunks. For example, if they want to save $50 for a toy, help them figure out how much they need to save each week. Provide them with a step-by-step guide for tracking their savings, such as a weekly log where they can record their progress. This process not only teaches them about saving but also about planning and setting realistic targets.

Success stories and real-life examples can be powerful motivators for children. Take the story of Emily, a young girl who wanted to buy a new bike. Her parents encouraged her to save a portion of her weekly allowance for the bike. They set up a savings jar and a chart to track her progress. Over several months, Emily diligently saved her money, and eventually, she had enough to buy the bike. The pride and satisfaction she felt when she finally purchased it were immense. Emily's parents shared that this experience taught her the value of saving and delayed gratification, lessons that continue to benefit her as she grows older.

Another inspiring example is the case of the Albert siblings, Jack and Lily. Their parents introduced a savings challenge where the kids had to save for a family trip to the zoo. Each week, Jack and Lily set aside a portion of their allowance in their savings jars. They even did extra chores to earn more money. The visual progress of their savings jars filling up kept them motivated. By the time they had saved enough for the trip, they were not only excited about the outing but also proud of their achievement. Testimonials from their parents highlight how this experience instilled a sense of responsibility and the importance of working towards a goal.

Teaching children to save is about more than just putting money aside. It's about instilling values of responsibility, planning, and delayed gratification. By making saving fun and rewarding, setting specific goals, and sharing success stories, you can help your child develop habits that will serve them well into adulthood. These early lessons in saving lay the groundwork for a financially stable and successful future.

6.4 Introducing Investment Concepts to Teens

Teaching teens about investing can be a game-changer for their financial future. Early exposure to investing not only demystifies the process but also sets the stage for long-term financial success. Imagine your teen learning about compound interest and realizing that a small investment today can grow exponentially over time. The power of compound interest is profound. For example, if a teen starts investing $100 a month at age 16 with an average annual return of 7%, they could have over $250,000 by the time they're 60. This illustrates the importance of starting early and letting time work in their favor.

Introducing basic investment concepts to teens doesn't have to be complicated. Start by explaining the difference between stocks, bonds, and mutual funds. Stocks represent ownership in a company. When someone buys a stock, they own a piece of that company and have a claim on part of its assets and earnings. Bonds, on the other hand, are loans made to corporations or governments. When you buy a bond, you're lending money in exchange for regular interest payments and the return of the principal at maturity. Mutual funds pool money from many investors to buy a diversified portfolio of stocks, bonds, or other securities. This diversification helps spread risk.

Next, explain how the stock market works. The stock market is where shares of publicly traded companies are bought and sold. It's a marketplace where investors can buy a piece of a company and potentially benefit from its growth. The prices of stocks fluctuate based on supply and demand, company performance, and broader economic factors. Understanding these basics helps teens grasp the bigger picture of investing and how their money can grow over time.

Practical ways for teens to start investing can make the process more accessible. Setting up a custodial account with parental guidance is a great starting point. These accounts allow teens to invest in stocks, bonds, and mutual funds while parents maintain control until the child reaches adulthood. It's a hands-on way for teens to learn about investing in a controlled environment. Additionally, investment apps designed for teens can simplify the process. Apps like Stockpile and Raiz are user-friendly and educational, making it easy for teens to start investing with small amounts of money. These platforms often include educational resources, helping teens understand their investments and track their progress.

Real-life examples and success stories can inspire teens to take their first steps into investing. Consider the story of Alex, a teenager who started investing with his parents' guidance. Alex set up a custodial account and chose to invest in companies he was familiar with, like Apple and Google. Over time, he saw his investments grow and learned valuable lessons about the stock market. Alex's parents shared that this experience taught him patience, the importance of research, and the benefits of long-term investing. It also meant he could get dividends from the companies he invested in further accelerating his return.

Another inspiring example is Maya, who started investing at 15 with the help of an investment app. Maya used Stockpile to buy fractional shares of her favorite companies. By investing small amounts regularly, she built a diversified portfolio. Maya's parents encouraged her to track her investments and learn about the companies she invested in. This hands-on experience gave her a deeper understanding of the stock market and the confidence to make informed financial decisions. Today, Maya is a financially savvy young adult, thanks to the early introduction to investing.

Testimonials from parents and teens highlight the transformative power of early investing. Parents often share how their teens became more interested in financial news and more disciplined in their spending and saving habits. Teens express a sense of empowerment and excitement about growing their money. These stories reinforce the idea that early exposure to investing can lay a strong foundation for financial independence and success.

Teaching teens about investing equips them with the knowledge and skills to build a secure financial future. By explaining basic concepts, offering practical ways to start, and sharing real-life success stories, you can help your teen navigate the world of investing with confidence and enthusiasm.

6.5 Resources and Tools for Family Financial Education

When it comes to teaching financial literacy, having the right resources can make a world of difference. Books, websites, and apps specifically designed for different age groups can help you provide the education your children need. For young kids, books like "The Berenstain Bears Trouble with Money" offer simple yet effective lessons. These stories are engaging and make complex ideas like earning, saving, and spending accessible. As children get older, books like "Rich Dad Poor Dad for Teens" can offer a deeper understanding of financial principles. This book breaks down essential concepts in a way that teens can relate to, making it a useful resource for older kids.

Educational websites and online games are also great tools for financial education. Websites like Jump$tart and Money As You Grow offer a wealth of resources, including articles, activities, and lesson plans tailored to different age groups. These sites make it easy to find age-appropriate content that aligns with what you want to teach. Online games like those found on OppU's website can turn learning into a fun activity. For younger children, games like

"Peter Pig's Money Counter" teach them to identify and count money, while older kids can benefit from more complex games like "Financial Football," which combines financial literacy with sports.

Using technology in financial education has numerous benefits. Apps and online tools can make learning more interactive and engaging. Budgeting apps designed for kids and teens, like PiggyBot and FamZoo, allow them to track their spending, set savings goals, and learn about budgeting in a hands-on way. These apps often include features that let you assign chores, track progress, and even pay allowances, making financial management a part of their daily routine. Interactive financial literacy games offer another layer of engagement, helping kids understand complex financial concepts through gameplay. These tools make learning about money feel less like a chore and more like an exciting challenge.

Integrating financial education into daily life can make these lessons more practical and impactful. Involve your children in family financial discussions. Let them see how you budget for groceries, plan for vacations, or save for big purchases. Use everyday activities as teaching moments. For example, when you're at the store, show them how to compare prices and use coupons. When planning a family vacation, explain how you budget for the trip and save money in advance. These real-life applications make financial concepts tangible and relevant, helping your children understand the importance of good money management.

Real-life examples of families using these resources can be incredibly inspiring. Take the case of the Pablo family. They used a mix of books, apps, and interactive games to teach their children about money. They started with simple books when their kids were young and gradually introduced more complex concepts as they grew older. The children used budgeting apps to manage their allowances and played online games that taught them about saving and investing. As a result, both kids developed a strong understanding of financial principles and are now confident in managing their own money.

Another example is the Patel family. They incorporated financial education into their daily routine by involving their children in financial decisions. The kids helped plan grocery trips, using apps to compare prices and find deals.

They also participated in family monthly Money meetings, where they learned about setting financial goals and tracking expenses. Their parents used online resources to supplement these lessons, providing a well-rounded financial education. Testimonials from the Patels highlight how these practices helped their children become more financially aware and responsible.

By leveraging a variety of resources, from books and websites to apps and games, you can provide a comprehensive financial education for your children. Using technology enhances learning, making it interactive and engaging. Integrating financial lessons into daily life ensures that these concepts are practical and relevant. Real-life examples show the positive impact of these practices, inspiring you to take similar steps with your own family. Teaching financial literacy is a journey, but with the right tools and strategies, you can set your children up for a lifetime of financial success.

Don't move on to the next chapter without doing the following;

1. If you have children, decide how you want to raise your kids with regard to allowances and money education. It's important to be on the same page. Have that conversation
2. If you don't have kids, lucky you, you will be much better off financially than those of us who have children!
3. Read your children money books
4. At the right age give them an allowance for chores
5. Download allowance apps like PiggyBot and FamZoo
6. Help your older children set up bank accounts, researching fees and interest rates
7. Set up custodial investment accounts and teach them the basic investment fundamentals

Chapter 7

Tax Planning and Maximizing Savings

Imagine you're sitting down at the kitchen table, a stack of tax forms and receipts spread out in front of you. Your kids are playing in the next room, and you can't help but feel a twinge of anxiety about whether you're handling your family's taxes correctly. It's a common scenario, but understanding the basics of tax planning can transform this stressful moment into a manageable task that benefits your whole family.

7.1 Understanding Your Tax Bracket

In the United States, the tax system is progressive, meaning that different portions of your income are taxed at different rates. This system is designed to ensure that those with higher incomes pay a higher percentage in taxes. For instance, if you earn $50,000 a year, your income isn't taxed at a flat rate. Instead, it's divided into segments, with each segment taxed at a progressively higher rate. The first portion might be taxed at 10%, the next at 12%, and so on. This layered approach means that as your income increases, only the income within the higher bracket is taxed at the higher rate, not your entire income.

To illustrate, let's say you're a single filer making $50,000 a year. According to the IRS, the first $11,000 is taxed at 10%, the next $33,725 at 12%, and the remaining $5,275 at 22%. So, your tax bill isn't a simple percentage of $50,000 but a sum of smaller percentages applied to portions of your income. This progressive system helps to balance the tax burden more fairly across different income levels. Understanding this can help you see how your take-home pay is affected.

Knowing your tax bracket can significantly inform your financial decisions. For instance, if you're planning to take on a side gig or overtime work, understanding your tax bracket can help you calculate how much of that extra income you'll keep after taxes. This knowledge empowers you to make more informed decisions about your work and investments, ensuring you maximize your take-home pay and if freelancing save enough for tax.

To provide a clearer picture, let's look at some sample calculations. If you have a gross income of $80,000, your net income—what you take home after taxes—will be significantly less. Using the 2023 tax rates, the first $22,000 for a married couple filing jointly is taxed at 10%, the next $67,450 at 12%, and so on. By breaking it down, you can see how each portion of your income is taxed at different rates, giving you a clearer understanding of your actual earnings.

Knowing your tax bracket also helps in planning for potential raises or bonuses. If you're considering a job offer that includes a significant salary increase, understanding how the new salary fits into your tax bracket can help you negotiate better. For example, you might ask for additional benefits like health insurance or retirement contributions, which aren't taxed as income, instead of a higher salary that would push you into a higher tax bracket. This strategic planning can help you make the most of your earnings.

Several tools and resources can help you determine your tax bracket and plan accordingly. Online tax calculators, such as those offered by the IRS or financial websites like TurboTax, can provide a quick and easy way to see where you fall within the tax brackets. These calculators can also help you estimate your tax liability, making it easier to plan your finances throughout the year. By inputting your income and other relevant details, you can get

CHAPTER 7

an accurate picture of your tax situation, helping you make more informed financial decisions.

Understanding your tax bracket is a crucial aspect of tax planning. It helps you see how your income is taxed, informs your financial decisions, and allows you to strategize effectively. With the right tools and knowledge, you can navigate the tax system more confidently, ensuring you make the most of your hard-earned money.

7.2 Utilizing Tax-Advantaged Accounts

Tax-advantaged accounts are a fantastic way to save money while also reducing your taxable income. These accounts come in various forms, each offering unique benefits tailored to different financial needs. Common types include the 401(k), Traditional IRA, Roth IRA, Health Savings Account (HSA), and 529 College Savings Plan. Understanding how these accounts work can help you make the most of your savings and investments.

Starting with the 401(k), this is an employer-sponsored retirement plan that allows you to contribute pre-tax dollars, reducing your taxable income for the year. The money in your 401(k) grows tax-deferred, meaning you don't pay taxes on the gains until you withdraw the funds during retirement. Many employers also offer matching contributions, which are essentially free money added to your retirement savings. For example, if your employer matches up to 5% of your salary, and you earn $60,000 a year, you could receive an additional $3,000 in matching funds.

Traditional IRAs work similarly by allowing pre-tax contributions. Like the 401(k), the money grows tax-deferred, and you pay taxes upon withdrawal. This can be particularly beneficial if you expect to be in a lower tax bracket during retirement. On the other hand, Roth IRAs offer a different advantage. Contributions to a Roth IRA are made with after-tax dollars, but the growth and withdrawals are tax-free, provided certain conditions are met. This makes Roth IRAs an excellent choice if you anticipate being in a higher tax bracket when you retire. For instance, if you contribute $5,000 to a Roth IRA every year for 30 years, and it grows to $500,000, all that growth is tax-free when you withdraw it in retirement.

Health Savings Accounts (HSAs) are another powerful tool, especially if you have a high-deductible health plan. Contributions to an HSA are tax-deductible i.e. you are not taxed on your contributions, the money grows tax-free, and withdrawals for qualified medical expenses are also tax-free. This triple tax advantage makes HSAs incredibly valuable. Additionally, after age 65, you can use HSA funds for non-medical expenses without penalty, although such withdrawals will be taxed as ordinary income. This flexibility makes HSAs not only a tool for current healthcare costs but also a secondary retirement account. These can be opened with some employers and contributions taken as part of your pay packet or you can contribute yourself through a brokerage.

The 529 College Savings Plan is tailored for educational expenses. Contributions are made with after-tax dollars, but the growth is tax-free, and withdrawals for qualified educational expenses are also tax-free. This makes 529 plans an excellent choice for saving for your children's college tuition, books, and other educational costs. For example, if you start contributing $200 a month to a 529 plan when your child is born, you could accumulate a significant amount by the time they're ready for college, all of which can be used tax-free for their education.

Choosing the right tax-advantaged account depends on your specific needs and goals. If you're focused on retirement, consider the benefits of Traditional vs. Roth IRAs based on your current and expected future tax brackets. If healthcare costs are a concern, an HSA can be a great addition to your financial toolkit. For educational goals, a 529 plan is a smart choice. Comparing these options helps you make informed decisions that align with your financial situation and future plans.

Setting up and contributing to these accounts is straightforward. To open an account, you can visit a financial institution, such as a bank or brokerage firm, and fill out the necessary paperwork. Many employers also offer 401(k) plans that you can enroll in through your human resources department as well as HSAs. Once your account is set up, consider setting up automatic contributions from your paycheck. This ensures that you're consistently saving without having to think about it. For instance, you might decide to contribute 10% of your salary to your 401(k) or set up a monthly transfer to your IRA or HSA. Automated contributions make it easier to stay on track with your savings goals, providing peace of mind and financial security.

7.3 Strategies for Minimizing Tax Liabilities

Tax planning isn't something you tackle just once a year; it's an ongoing process that can significantly impact your financial well-being. Regularly reviewing your financial status and making adjustments as needed throughout the year can help you minimize your tax liabilities and make the most of your hard-earned money. This proactive approach ensures that you're not scrambling at the last minute, trying to find deductions or credits to lower your tax bill. Instead, you're consistently making informed financial decisions that keep your taxes in check.

One of the most effective strategies to reduce taxable income is maximizing contributions to tax-advantaged accounts. By contributing to accounts like a 401(k), Traditional IRA, or Health Savings Account (HSA), you can lower your taxable income for the year. For example, if you contribute $6,500 to a Traditional IRA, that amount is deducted from your taxable income, potentially moving you into a lower tax bracket. Similarly, contributing to an HSA not only reduces your taxable income but also provides a tax-free way to pay for qualified medical expenses. These contributions are a win-win, helping you save for the future while reducing your current tax burden.

Taking advantage of employer benefits, such as Flexible Spending Accounts (FSAs), is another excellent way to minimize taxes. FSAs allow you to set aside pre-tax dollars to pay for eligible healthcare and dependent care expenses. This means you don't pay taxes on the money you contribute to the FSA, effectively lowering your taxable income. For instance, if you set aside $2,500 in an FSA for healthcare expenses, you're not taxed on that amount, providing significant savings over the year. It's a simple yet effective way to manage both your healthcare costs and your tax liabilities.

Making charitable contributions can also provide valuable tax benefits. Donations to qualified charitable organizations can be deducted from your taxable income, reducing your overall tax liability. Whether you're donating cash, goods, or even appreciated assets like stocks, these contributions can make a big difference. Donating appreciated assets, such as stocks that have increased in value, offers a dual benefit: you avoid paying capital gains tax on the appreciation, and you get a deduction for the full market value of the asset. For instance, if you donate stock worth $5,000 that you originally purchased for $3,000, you avoid the capital gains tax on the $2,000 gain and receive a $5,000 deduction.

Keeping detailed records of your charitable contributions is crucial for claiming these deductions. Ensure you have receipts or written acknowledgments from the charitable organizations, especially for contributions over $250. These records will be necessary when filing your taxes and can help you substantiate your deductions if you're ever audited.

By implementing these strategies—maximizing contributions to tax-advantaged accounts, utilizing FSAs, and making charitable contributions—you can significantly reduce your taxable income and pay less tax. If you are paying down debt, don't focus on these strategies just yet; cycle back to these once your debt is paid off. Regularly reviewing your financial status and making strategic adjustments throughout the year ensures that you're always in the best position to minimize your tax liabilities.

7.4 Planning for Tax Season

Imagine it's late March, and you're scrambling to gather all your tax documents, unsure if you've missed any crucial forms or receipts. The stress of tax season is all too familiar for many families, but with a bit of preparation, you can turn this chaotic time into a smooth, manageable process. Being prepared for tax season not only reduces stress but also minimizes errors that could cost you money or trigger an audit.

Start by creating a checklist of necessary documents and information. This list should include W-2s, 1099s, mortgage interest statements, medical expenses, charitable donation receipts, and any other relevant documents. Having a comprehensive checklist ensures that you won't overlook any important paperwork. Set up a dedicated space for tax documents throughout the year, such as a specific drawer or folder. As soon as you receive any tax-related documents, place them in this designated space. This habit will save you time and reduce last-minute scrambling.

A month-by-month guide can help you stay on track with tax preparation tasks. In January, focus on gathering all your income statements, such as W-2s and 1099s. These forms typically arrive by the end of the month, so keep an eye on your mailbox and email. February is the time to organize receipts and documentation for deductions. Sort through your medical bills, charitable donations, and any other deductible expenses. This organization will make it easier to input data into tax software or spreadsheets and provide it to your tax professional. By March, schedule a meeting with a tax professional if needed. Whether you're dealing with complex tax situations or just want peace of mind, a professional can provide valuable guidance and ensure accuracy.

Using tax software or hiring a professional can make tax season more manageable. Tax software options like TurboTax, H&R Block, and TaxAct offer user-friendly interfaces and step-by-step instructions. These programs can automatically import your W-2s and 1099s, saving you time and reducing the chance of errors. They also provide guidance on deductions and credits you might otherwise overlook. Compare these options based on your needs and budget to find the best fit. For more complex tax situations, consider hiring a CPA or tax advisor. Professionals can offer personalized advice, help you navigate complicated tax laws, and represent you in case of an audit. If you're unsure which route to take, consider starting with tax software and upgrading to professional help if you encounter issues.

Avoiding common tax season mistakes can save you time and money. Double-checking Social Security numbers and other personal information is crucial. A simple typo can delay your refund or cause other issues. Make sure all names, addresses, and identification numbers are accurate. Reviewing last year's tax return can also provide valuable insights. Look for missed deductions or credits that you can claim this year. This review can also help you catch any changes in your financial situation that might affect your current return. For example, if you started a side gig or had a significant medical expense, these changes could impact your deductions and credits.

Finally, keeping detailed records throughout the year can simplify the entire process. Regularly update your checklist with new documents as they come in. This ongoing organization ensures that you have everything you need when it's time to file. Additionally, consider using financial management apps that can help you track expenses and categorize transactions. These tools can provide detailed reports, making it easier to identify deductible expenses and gather the necessary documentation.

Planning for tax season involves more than just scrambling to file your return in April. By creating a checklist, setting up a dedicated space for documents, and following a month-by-month guide, you can stay organized and reduce stress. Using tax software or hiring a professional can further simplify the process and ensure accuracy. Avoiding common mistakes by double-checking information and reviewing past returns can save you time and money. With a bit of preparation and ongoing organization, tax season can become a manageable and even predictable part of your financial routine.

7.5 Common Tax Deductions and Credits for Families

Understanding tax deductions and credits can help you save a significant amount of money on your tax bill. Deductions and credits work differently but both reduce the amount of tax you owe, albeit in different ways. Tax deductions reduce your taxable income. For instance, if you have $5,000 in deductions and your taxable income is $50,000, your taxable income becomes $45,000. On the other hand, tax credits reduce your tax owed dollar-for-dollar. So, if you owe $3,000 in taxes and you have $1,000 in credits, your tax bill drops to $2,000. This direct reduction makes credits particularly valuable.

There are several common deductions that can significantly reduce your taxable income. One of the most substantial is the mortgage interest deduction. If you own a home, you can deduct the interest paid on your mortgage, lowering your taxable income. For example, if you paid $10,000 in mortgage interest, that amount can be deducted, reducing your taxable income by the same amount. Another valuable deduction is the State and Local Taxes (SALT) deduction, which allows you to deduct state and local income, sales, and property taxes. However, this deduction is capped at $10,000. If you live in a state with high property taxes, this deduction can provide considerable relief. Medical expenses can also be deducted, but only if they exceed 7.5% of your adjusted gross income. This includes costs for medical care, prescriptions, and even some long-term care expenses. Keeping detailed records of these expenses is crucial to ensure you can claim them accurately.

Tax credits offer even more direct savings, and several are particularly beneficial for families. The Child Tax Credit, for instance, provides up to $2,000 per qualifying child under the age of 17. This credit is partially refundable, meaning if the credit exceeds your tax liability, you can receive up to $1,400 as a refund. The Earned Income Tax Credit (EITC) is another valuable credit that supports low to moderate-income working families. The amount varies based on income and the number of qualifying children, but it can provide a substantial refund. For example, a family with three or more children can receive a credit of up to $6,728. The Child and Dependent Care Credit helps families offset the cost of childcare or dependent care. If you pay for care so you can work or look for work, you can claim up to 35% of $3,000 in care expenses for one child or $6,000 for two or more, providing a maximum credit of $2,100.

Qualifying for and claiming these deductions and credits requires careful record-keeping and adherence to IRS guidelines. To qualify for the Child Tax Credit, your child must have a valid Social Security number, live with you for more than half the year, and not provide more than half of their own support. Documentation, such as birth certificates and Social Security cards, should be kept handy. For the EITC, you must meet income requirements and file a tax return, even if you don't owe any taxes. The IRS website offers tools to help determine your eligibility. The Child and Dependent Care Credit requires you to provide the care provider's name, address, and taxpayer identification number. Keep receipts and records of all payments made for care services.

Claiming these deductions and credits on your tax return involves a few steps. First, gather all necessary documents, such as W-2s, 1099s, mortgage interest statements, and receipts for deductible expenses. Use tax software or consult a tax professional to ensure you enter the information correctly. For deductions, itemize them on Schedule A of Form 1040. For credits like the Child Tax Credit and EITC, follow the instructions on the relevant sections of Form 1040. Detailed records and accurate filing can maximize your savings and ensure compliance with tax laws.

Understanding and utilizing tax deductions and credits can greatly reduce your tax liability and increase your refund. By knowing the differences between deductions and credits, identifying common deductions, and leveraging valuable tax credits, you can make informed decisions that benefit your family's financial health. Proper documentation and careful filing are essential to claim these benefits accurately. I think the fee you pay a professional to file taxes on your behalf is a worthwhile investment. They will claim things you would never know about yourself, so I think it's worth the money.

If you are due a tax refund, what should you do with it? I hate to sound boring, but if you have debt, you should pay down your debt first. It will make a massive difference to the length of time needed to pay down the remaining balance and help you repay your debt sooner. If your debt is paid off, then next is to add to your emergency fund. If you're saving for a house deposit, then this is a great lump sum that can help. As you've read, being a homeowner has significant tax advantages, so getting you into a home as soon as you can makes great financial sense. If all of those savings goals have been met then the money is all yours to do with what you choose - consider a vacation or treat yourself to something, after all, you earned it!

CHAPTER 7

7.6 Long-term Tax Planning Strategies

Long-term tax planning is like planting a tree. The earlier you start, the more time your efforts have to grow, providing shade and fruit for years to come. Proactive tax planning can lead to substantial savings over time, allowing you to make the most of your income and investments. Starting your tax planning early in the year gives you the advantage of time. It allows you to make adjustments as needed, rather than scrambling at the last minute. This approach fits seamlessly into overall financial planning, ensuring that tax considerations are integrated into your broader financial goals.

Major life events can have a significant impact on your taxes, and planning for these events can help you navigate the tax implications smoothly. For example, marriage can affect your tax situation in various ways. Filing jointly as a married couple can provide tax benefits, such as a higher standard deduction and potentially lower tax rates. However, it can also lead to the "marriage penalty," where your combined income pushes you into a higher tax bracket. It's important to evaluate both options—filing jointly and separately—to determine which is more advantageous for your situation. Similarly, having children introduces new tax benefits, such as the Child Tax Credit and additional exemptions. Planning for these benefits and adjusting your withholding accordingly can ensure you maximize your tax savings.

Buying a home is another major event that can affect your taxes. Mortgage interest and property taxes are deductible expenses, which can reduce your taxable income. Additionally, first-time home buyers may qualify for specific credits and deductions. Retiring also brings significant tax considerations. Withdrawals from retirement accounts, Social Security benefits, and potential changes in filing status all need careful planning. Adjusting your withholding and estimated tax payments after such major life changes ensures that you remain compliant and avoid unexpected tax bills.

To help implement these long-term tax planning strategies, a variety of tools and resources are available. Tax planning software, such as TurboTax and H&R Block, offers features that allow you to project future tax liabilities and explore different scenarios. These tools can help you see the potential impact of various strategies, making it easier to plan ahead. Financial planning worksheets and calculators can also be useful. They provide a structured way to assess your financial situation, set goals, and track your progress. By using these resources, you can take a proactive approach to tax planning, ensuring that you make informed decisions that benefit your financial health in the long run.

Long-term tax planning is essential for maximizing your financial well-being. By starting early, considering strategies like Roth IRA conversions, timing income and deductions, and planning for major life events, you can significantly reduce your tax liabilities. Utilize available tools and resources to implement these strategies effectively, ensuring that your tax planning fits seamlessly into your overall financial goals. This proactive approach not only saves you money but also provides peace of mind, knowing that you're prepared for whatever financial challenges come your way.

Don't move on to the next chapter without doing the following;

1. Decide how you are going to track your tax information. Will it be manually in a folder or spreadsheet or software like H&R Block or TurboTax
2. Start the spreadsheet or buy the tax software. Track your expenses and deductions
3. Meet with your personnel department to understand all the deductions you have available to you
4. Start making those deductions if you can afford to. Pay down debt first, then do these deductions once you are debt-free
5. File your tax return

In the next chapter, we'll explore how to build wealth by overcoming psychological barriers and developing a healthy money mindset.

Chapter 8

Overcoming Psychological Barriers and Building Wealth

Imagine this: You're at the checkout line at the grocery store, and as you swipe your card, you silently hope it goes through. You've been avoiding looking at your bank account, fearing what you'll find. This moment of dread is all too common, and it highlights a crucial aspect of financial success—overcoming psychological barriers. Understanding the mental hurdles that prevent you from achieving financial stability is the first step toward building wealth and peace of mind.

8.1 Recognizing Psychological Barriers to Financial Success

Many psychological barriers can hinder your financial progress. One of the most significant is the fear of failure and risk. This fear can paralyze you, making you hesitant to invest or take steps that could improve your financial situation. You might think, "What if I lose money?" or "What if I make the same mistakes again?" These fears are valid but can be debilitating if not addressed. For example, Kristi, a mom who faced significant financial fears, found herself stuck because she was afraid of repeating past mistakes. She feared being kicked out of her apartment and not setting a good example for her son.

Impulse buying due to emotional triggers is another common barrier. When you're stressed, sad, or even celebrating, you might find yourself making unnecessary purchases. These small buys can add up, draining your finances without you even realizing it. Procrastination and avoidance of financial tasks are also significant hurdles. You might avoid paying bills or checking your bank account because it feels overwhelming. This avoidance leads to bigger problems down the line, creating a cycle of stress and financial instability.

Financial stress can severely impact your decision-making. When you're stressed about money, you're more likely to make impulsive decisions, like taking out a payday loan or making a large, unnecessary purchase. This cycle of stress, leading to impulsive decisions, can be hard to break. Financial stress doesn't just affect you; it impacts your entire family. Arguments about money can strain relationships, and the constant worry can create a tense home environment. In these moments, it's crucial to reach out to family or support groups. Sharing your struggles can provide relief, and you might find that others have valuable advice or resources to help you.

To start overcoming these barriers, self-assessment is crucial. Reflect on your financial behavior and identify the patterns that hold you back. Self-reflection exercises can help you understand why you make certain financial decisions. For instance, keep a journal of your spending habits and note the emotions you feel when making purchases. Financial behavior quizzes are another useful tool. These quizzes can highlight areas where you might need to change your approach to money. They can also offer insights into your financial strengths and weaknesses, helping you develop a more effective strategy.

Real-life examples can be incredibly inspiring when tackling psychological barriers. Consider the story of a family who turned their financial situation around by addressing their fears and changing their habits. They started by creating a realistic budget and gradually built an emergency fund. By setting small, achievable goals, they gained confidence and broke free from their negative financial habits. Testimonials from individuals who overcame financial fears can also be motivating. Hearing how others faced similar struggles and emerged successful can give you the encouragement you need to take the first step.

Kristi's story is a powerful example of overcoming financial fears. She faced significant financial instability and was behind on filing her taxes due to a withholding error. By breaking down the task of filing past tax returns into smaller, manageable steps, she was able to tackle the problem without feeling overwhelmed. Kristi successfully filed her past tax returns, received refunds, and used the money to repay family loans. She also faced collection agencies by verifying debts, understanding her rights, and negotiating settlements. Today, Kristi maintains a budget, has an emergency fund, and continues to work toward her financial goals.

Recognizing and addressing psychological barriers is essential for financial success. Fear of failure, impulse buying, and procrastination can hold you back, but understanding these barriers and taking steps to overcome them can set you on the path to financial stability. By reflecting on your financial behavior, seeking support, and learning from real-life examples, you can break free from negative patterns and build the wealth and security your family deserves.

8.2 Developing a Healthy Money Mindset

A positive money mindset is crucial for financial success. Imagine waking up each morning with a sense of optimism about your financial future. This outlook can change how you handle money, making you more proactive and less fearful. The difference between a scarcity mindset and an abundance mindset is profound. A scarcity mindset focuses on limitations and fears, believing that there is never enough. This mindset often leads to hoarding money or avoiding investments out of fear. Conversely, an abundance mindset sees opportunities and believes in growth. It encourages you to take calculated risks, invest wisely, and believe in the possibility of financial success.

Your attitude towards money significantly influences your financial behavior. When you adopt a positive mindset, you're more likely to make choices that benefit your long-term financial health. For instance, instead of seeing a budget as a restriction, you view it as a tool for achieving your goals. This shift in perspective can lead to better financial decisions, like saving more consistently or investing in opportunities that align with your objectives. A positive money mindset also reduces stress, making it easier to handle financial setbacks. Instead of panicking, you trust that you can overcome challenges and continue progressing.

Shifting to a healthy money mindset involves practical steps that can transform negative thinking patterns. Start with daily affirmations and positive self-talk. Simple phrases like "I am capable of managing my finances" or "Every dollar I save brings me closer to my goals" can reinforce a positive outlook. Visualization exercises are another powerful tool. Spend a few minutes each day imagining your financial success, whether it's paying off debt, buying a home, or saving for retirement. Visualizing these outcomes makes them feel more attainable, motivating you to take the necessary steps to achieve them.

Gratitude plays a significant role in financial well-being. When you focus on what you have rather than what you lack, your financial outlook improves. Keeping a gratitude journal can be a helpful practice. Each day, write down a few things you're thankful for, especially those related to your finances. It could be as simple as having a steady job, being able to pay bills on time, or saving a small amount each month. This practice shifts your focus from scarcity to abundance, highlighting the positive aspects of your financial situation. Over time, this shift can reduce financial stress and increase your overall sense of well-being.

Real-life examples of mindset transformation can illustrate the power of a healthy money mindset. Consider the story of Mark, who struggled with a scarcity mindset for years. He constantly worried about money, avoided investing, and hoarded his savings. After learning about the abundance mindset, he began practicing daily affirmations and visualization exercises. Gradually, his outlook changed. He started investing in low-risk opportunities, created a budget that aligned with his goals, and saw his savings grow. This transformation didn't happen overnight, but the shift in mindset was the catalyst for his financial success.

Families can also benefit significantly from adopting an abundance mindset. Take the Adams family, for example. They used to view money as a source of stress and conflict. By focusing on gratitude and positive financial habits, they changed their perspective. They began involving their children in financial discussions, teaching them the value of saving and investing. Over time, their financial situation improved, and they achieved significant milestones like paying off debt and saving for college. This mindset shift created a more positive and collaborative family dynamic, aligning everyone's efforts toward common financial goals.

Developing a healthy money mindset is essential for achieving financial success. By understanding the difference between a scarcity and an abundance mindset, you can shift your perspective and make better financial decisions. Practical steps like daily affirmations, visualization exercises, and gratitude practices can transform your outlook. Real-life examples show that these changes are not just theoretical but can lead to substantial financial growth and stability for individuals and families alike.

8.3 Overcoming Fear and Anxiety About Money

Imagine staring at a financial statement, feeling a knot of anxiety tightening in your chest. You're not alone. Many families grapple with financial fears that can hinder progress. One of the most common fears is the fear of investing and losing money. This fear can paralyze you, making you hesitant to put your money into anything that carries risk. You might think, "What if the market crashes?" or "What if I make the wrong investment?" These worries are understandable, especially if you've faced financial setbacks before. Anxiety about debt and financial instability is another significant barrier. The thought of mounting debt can be overwhelming, leading you to avoid dealing with it altogether. This avoidance only exacerbates the problem, creating a cycle of stress and financial instability.

Fear and anxiety can significantly impact your financial decisions, often leading to inaction or poor choices. When you're constantly worried about money, it's easy to miss out on investment opportunities that could grow your wealth. For instance, many people avoid investing in the stock market because they fear losing their savings. This fear can result in missed opportunities for significant financial growth. The psychological toll of constant financial worry is immense. It can affect your sleep, your relationships, and your overall well-being. When you're stressed about money, it's hard to think clearly and make rational decisions. This stress can lead to impulsive choices, like taking out high-interest loans or making unnecessary purchases, which only worsen your financial situation.

To manage and overcome these fears, consider adopting mindfulness and relaxation techniques. Mindfulness involves staying present and focused on the current moment, which can help reduce anxiety. Simple practices like deep breathing exercises or guided meditations can make a big difference. These techniques can help you stay calm and focused, making it easier to tackle financial tasks without feeling overwhelmed. Seeking professional help, such as financial therapy or counseling, can also be beneficial. A financial therapist can help you understand the root causes of your financial fears and develop strategies to overcome them. They can provide a safe space to discuss your anxieties and offer practical advice for managing your finances more effectively.

Real-life examples can provide inspiration and motivation. Consider the story of Tom, who was paralyzed by the fear of investing due to a previous financial loss. After seeking help from a financial counselor, he learned to manage his anxiety and started investing small amounts in low-risk options. Over time, his confidence grew, and so did his investments. Another example is the Lopez family, who faced significant anxiety about their mounting debt. They sought the help of a financial advisor who helped them create a realistic budget and debt repayment plan. By taking small, manageable steps, they gradually reduced their debt and alleviated their anxiety. These stories show that overcoming financial fears is possible with the right support and strategies.

CHAPTER 8

Financial fears can hold you back, but they don't have to define your financial future. Let me repeat this as it's really important, **Financial fears can hold you back, but they don't have to define your financial future**. By recognizing and addressing your fears, you can take control of your finances and build a more secure future for your family. Mindfulness and professional help are valuable tools in managing anxiety, and real-life stories show that overcoming these fears is achievable.

8.4 Building Financial Confidence Through Education

Education plays a pivotal role in building financial confidence. Think about the times you've felt assured because you knew exactly what you were doing. That same confidence can extend to your finances when you arm yourself with knowledge. Financial literacy directly correlates with confidence. When you understand how money works, you make better decisions, reducing the stress that often accompanies financial management. For instance, knowing the basics of compound interest can help you make informed investment choices while understanding how to budget can prevent you from living paycheck to paycheck.

Reducing financial stress through education is not just theoretical—it's practical and achievable. Take Sarah, for example. She used to panic every time a bill arrived. After taking an online personal finance course, she learned how to create a budget and manage her expenses. This knowledge transformed her financial life, turning stress into a sense of control. Educational resources can provide this transformation. Books like this one or courses on online platforms such as Coursera and Udemy have courses on personal finance that can be taken at your own pace. This book, as you read it, may seem overwhelming at first with a lot of new financial jargon you're not familiar with. You don't have to understand every detail straight away. Write down things you're going to do straight away and what you'll focus on later once you have the head space. Talk about it during your monthly Money nights and keep making progress in your money education. As you progress you'll find that your goals will change and become bigger than you first thought possible.

Continuous learning keeps you informed about financial matters, ensuring you stay ahead in managing your money. Joining financial literacy groups or forums can be incredibly beneficial. These communities provide support, answer questions, and share experiences. Attending seminars and workshops adds another layer of understanding. These events often feature experts who can offer insights and tips you might not find elsewhere. The power of passing on what you learn cannot be overstated. Teaching your children or discussing financial strategies with friends reinforces your knowledge and helps others improve their financial literacy.

Success stories of individuals who turned their finances around through learning can be incredibly inspiring. Take John, who was drowning in debt and felt hopeless. After enrolling in a financial literacy course, he learned how to create a repayment plan and budget effectively. Within two years, he paid off all his debt and started saving for a house. Testimonials from families who educated themselves and achieved financial stability offer a roadmap for what's possible. The Jeffrey family, for instance, attended financial workshops together and applied what they learned. They went from living paycheck to paycheck to having a robust savings account and a clear investment strategy.

Building financial confidence through education is about more than just reading a book or taking a course. It's about applying what you learn and continuously seeking new knowledge. This approach empowers you to make informed decisions, reduces financial stress, and builds a secure future for your family.

Education's role in financial confidence is undeniable. The correlation between financial literacy and confidence is clear: the more you know, the better decisions you can make. This knowledge reduces stress, transforming financial management from a source of anxiety to a source of empowerment. Resources for improving financial literacy are abundant. Recommended reading lists can guide you to books that offer practical advice, like "The Latte Factor" by David Bach or "Your Money or Your Life" by Vicki Robin.

The benefits of continuous learning are immense. Joining financial literacy groups or forums allows you to engage with others who share your goals, providing support and motivation. Attending seminars and workshops offers the chance to learn from experts and gain insights that can be applied to your financial strategy. Sharing what you learn with others not only reinforces your knowledge but also helps those around you improve their financial literacy.

Success stories highlight the transformative power of education. Consider Lisa, who was always stressed about money. After taking a budgeting course, she learned to manage her income and expenses effectively. This education gave her the confidence to start investing, and within a few years, she saw significant growth in her savings. Testimonials from families who achieved financial stability through education further illustrate these benefits. The Thompson family attended financial workshops and applied what they learned to their daily lives. They moved from financial insecurity to a place where they could comfortably save for their children's college education and their own retirement.

8.5 Creating a Wealth-Building Routine

Establishing a wealth-building routine can transform your financial future. Think of it as setting up a series of habits that, over time, lead to significant financial success. Consistency is key. Just like brushing your teeth daily keeps your dental health in check, regular financial habits maintain and grow your wealth. Simple daily actions, like tracking your expenses, can make a huge difference. Weekly routines, such as updating your budget, keep you on track. Monthly habits, like reviewing your investment performance, ensure you're meeting your financial goals. Each of these small actions, when done consistently, contributes to a stable and prosperous financial future.

Creating a wealth-building routine begins with setting clear financial goals. Start by identifying what you want to achieve. Are you saving for a down payment on a house? Planning for retirement? Or maybe you want to build an emergency fund? Write down your goals and break them into smaller, manageable steps. Track your progress regularly to stay motivated. Use a simple spreadsheet or a financial app to monitor your savings, expenses, and investments. This tracking helps you see where your money is going and allows you to make adjustments as needed. Regularly reviewing and adjusting your budget and investments ensures that you stay on course and adapt to any changes in your financial situation.

Automation plays a crucial role in wealth-building. By automating your savings and investments, you ensure consistency without having to think about it constantly. Set up automatic transfers from your checking account to your savings and investment accounts. This way, a portion of your income goes directly into building your wealth before you even have a chance to spend it. Financial apps can make this process even easier. Apps like Raiz or Oportun automatically save small amounts for you based on your spending patterns. They can also round up your purchases to the nearest dollar and invest the spare change. These automated systems help you build wealth effortlessly and consistently.

Real-life examples can illustrate the power of a wealth-building routine. Take the story of Lisa and Mark, a couple who decided to automate their savings and investments. They set up automatic transfers to their retirement accounts and savings for their children's education. Every month, a portion of their income went directly into these accounts without them having to lift a finger. Over the years, they watched their savings grow steadily. They also reviewed their budget during their monthly Money meetings, making adjustments as needed. This consistency paid off, allowing them to achieve their financial goals and build a secure future for their family.

Another inspiring example is the Foy family. They created a wealth-building routine that involved regular family meetings to discuss their financial goals and progress. They set clear goals, like paying off debt and saving for a vacation, and tracked their progress using a shared spreadsheet. They also automated their savings, ensuring that a portion of their income went into different savings and investment accounts each month. This routine helped them stay focused and motivated, and over time, they saw significant financial growth. Their consistent habits and clear goals transformed their financial situation, providing stability and peace of mind.

Creating a wealth-building routine is about establishing regular financial habits that lead to long-term success. Consistency in daily, weekly, and monthly actions like tracking expenses, updating budgets, and reviewing investments is key. Setting clear financial goals and automating savings and investments ensure that you stay on track without constant effort. Real-life examples, like those of Lisa and Mark or the Foy family, show how these routines can lead to significant financial growth and stability. By incorporating these habits into your daily life, you can build a secure and prosperous financial future for your family.

So here's my suggestion to you, set up a monthly money meeting with your spouse or family. Make it fun, cook a nice meal, and open a bottle of wine. In the early stages of these meetings, it will be creating budgets and getting clear on your goals, but once that is all done it's a check-in meeting. How is our budget tracking? Do we need to make any tweaks? We've got Christmas coming up so we need to be saving for that and maybe cutting back on something else to do that. Check how your investments are tracking. Do you need to sell anything or rebalance your portfolio? Are your automatic payments going through to your retirement accounts, college funds, or your emergency fund? How is your debt payment plan progressing? Can you accelerate it with the tax refund you got or by paying a larger repayment now that one credit card has been paid off? Check-in with your goals you set; are you on track to hit those goals? Do you need to adjust anything? Do you want to add new goals? Then celebrate all you have achieved. Before you started this journey you were in a worse position, now you have made significant progress to your financial future; cheers to that!

8.6 Celebrating Financial Milestones and Progress

Imagine the satisfaction of finally paying off a credit card that's been hanging over your head for years. Celebrating such milestones is more than just a pat on the back; it's a powerful motivator for continued progress. Recognizing your achievements can boost your morale and keep you focused on your financial goals. When you acknowledge your hard work, you reinforce positive financial behaviors, making it easier to stay committed to your plan. Celebrating achievements like reaching a savings goal, paying off a loan, or sticking to a budget for several months can provide the encouragement you need to keep going.

There are many creative and meaningful ways to celebrate financial milestones. Planning a family outing or special dinner can be a wonderful way to mark these achievements. For instance, if you've paid off a significant debt, consider treating your family to a day at the zoo or a favorite restaurant. This celebration doesn't have to be extravagant; the key is to make it memorable and enjoyable. Another idea is to set up a reward system for reaching financial goals. You can create a list of rewards for different milestones, such as a weekend getaway for hitting a major savings target or a new gadget for consistently sticking to your budget. If you're still paying off a lot of debt consider having a celebration like a picnic in the park or a day at the beach with friends. It doesn't need to be a lot, it's the concept of celebrating you should focus on and sharing it with others. These rewards can make the process of managing money more enjoyable and provide tangible incentives to stay on track.

Reflection plays a crucial role in financial growth. Taking the time to look back on your journey and learn from your experiences can provide valuable insights. Keeping a financial journal is an excellent way to track your progress and record lessons learned. You can jot down your achievements, challenges, and strategies that worked well. This journal becomes a personal guidebook that you can refer to whenever you need a boost of motivation or a reminder of how far you've come. Regularly reviewing and celebrating past successes also helps you stay focused on your goals. Set aside time each month or quarter to reflect on your financial achievements. This practice not only reinforces positive behaviors but also helps you identify areas for improvement.

Real-life examples can be incredibly motivating when it comes to celebrating financial milestones. Consider the story of the Anderson family. They had been struggling with debt for years but finally managed to pay off a significant portion through disciplined budgeting and saving. To celebrate, they planned a small family vacation, something they had put off for a long time. This celebration not only marked their achievement but also strengthened their resolve to continue their financial journey. Testimonials from individuals who celebrated their financial wins can also be inspiring. For instance, Sarah, a single mom, celebrated paying off her student loans by hosting a small dinner party for friends and family. This event was a way to share her success and thank those who supported her along the way.

Another powerful story is that of James, who used celebration as a tool for continued success. After reaching his savings goal for an emergency fund, he treated himself to a new pair of running shoes and signed up for a marathon. This personal reward not only celebrated his financial achievement but also encouraged him to set new goals, both financial and personal. By tying his financial success to something he was passionate about, James found additional motivation to maintain his positive financial habits.

Celebrating financial milestones is about more than just recognition; it's about motivating continued progress, reflecting on your journey, and learning from your experiences. Whether it's planning a family outing, setting up a reward system, or keeping a financial journal, these practices can reinforce positive financial behaviors and provide the encouragement needed to stay on track. Real-life examples and testimonials show that celebrating achievements can be a powerful tool for financial growth and stability. So, take the time to acknowledge your hard work and enjoy the journey to financial success.

By celebrating your financial wins, you create a positive cycle of motivation and progress. This chapter has highlighted the importance of recognizing achievements, offering creative ways to celebrate, and the benefits of reflection. As you move forward, remember that each milestone is a step closer to your financial goals. Next, we'll explore how to build a secure financial future for your family, focusing on strategies that ensure long-term stability and growth.

Don't move on to the next chapter without doing the following;

1. Download an app like Balance or Calm and listen to some meditations. It can take as little as 5 minutes to make a mindset shift that can last throughout the day
2. Consider journaling, whether it's a gratitude journal or just writing down how you're feeling, it's great to write it down
3. Decide if you should see a financial advisor, if you need help, it's a worthwhile investment
4. Set up your monthly Money meeting schedule and stick to it
5. Set up rewards for when you achieve milestones and celebrate!

Conclusion

As we come to the end of "**Financial Freedom Made Easy**" let's take a moment to reflect on the journey we've been on together. Financial literacy can seem overwhelming, but understanding the basics is crucial for building a secure future for your family. Remember, developing a healthy financial mindset is the foundation. Your beliefs about money shape your decisions, so set realistic financial goals and challenge any negative beliefs that hold you back.

Creating and sticking to a budget is your roadmap to financial stability. By mastering budgeting techniques, you can manage your finances, reduce unnecessary expenses, and build an emergency fund. It's not just about cutting costs but about making informed decisions that align with your family's values and goals. Start small, like saving $50 a month, and watch these habits grow into significant financial improvements over time.

Debt can feel like a heavy burden, but with strategies like the Debt Pay Down and Debt Accelerator methods, you can systematically eliminate it. Focus on paying off the smallest debts first for quick wins, or tackle high-interest debts to save on interest costs. Find what works best for you and stay committed. The freedom from debt will give you the breathing room to focus on other financial goals.

Investing might seem intimidating, but it's one of the most effective ways to build long-term wealth. Start with basic concepts like stocks, bonds, and mutual funds, and remember the importance of diversification. Low-cost index funds are a great starting point for families. They offer broad market exposure with minimal fees. The earlier you start investing, the more you can benefit from compound interest, growing your wealth over time.

Planning for retirement is essential. Calculate your needs, understand different retirement accounts, and implement long-term savings strategies.

It's not just about how much you save but how you save it. Contributing to tax-advantaged accounts can maximize your savings and provide a more secure future. Don't wait until it's too late; start planning now to ensure a comfortable retirement.

Teaching your children about money is one of the greatest gifts you can give them. Financial education should start early. Provide age-appropriate lessons and encourage good savings and investment habits. Use everyday scenarios to teach them about budgeting, saving, and the value of money. This will set them up for a lifetime of smart financial decisions.

Tax planning might not be the most exciting topic, but it's vital for maximizing your savings. Utilize tax-advantaged accounts, minimize liabilities, and keep organized records. Understanding your tax bracket and planning accordingly can make a significant difference in your take-home pay. Simple strategies like contributing to a retirement account or using an HSA can save you money in the long run.

We all face psychological barriers when it comes to money. Overcoming these barriers is crucial for financial success. Develop a positive money mindset and create wealth-building routines. Addressing fears and anxieties about money head-on can transform your financial decisions. Remember, it's okay to seek professional advice if you need personalized guidance. Financial therapists and advisors can provide valuable support and help you navigate complex financial situations.

Start small and build gradually. Set specific financial goals and track your progress. Utilize the apps and resources I've provided throughout this book. Don't hesitate to seek professional advice if needed. Financial success is a journey that requires persistence and resilience. Keep learning and adapting as you go.

I want to reaffirm your ability to succeed. With the right knowledge and tools, you can improve your financial situation. I've been where you are, feeling overwhelmed and unsure. But through trial and error, I've learned that financial stability is achievable. You have the power to change your financial future. Stay persistent, learn from your mistakes, and never give up.

As you move forward, express confidence in your future. You now have the knowledge to build a secure and prosperous financial future for yourself and your family. Remember, it's not about perfection but progress. Every step you take, no matter how small, brings you closer to your financial goals. I believe in you, and I'm confident that with the right mindset and strategies, you can achieve financial success.

Thank you for joining me on this journey. Here's to a brighter, more secure financial future for you and your family. I wish you every success.

* * *

<u>Make a Difference with Your Review</u>

People who give without expecting anything in return live happier lives. So, let's make a difference together!

Would you help someone just like you—curious about Financial Freedom but unsure where to start?

My mission is to make Financial Freedom understandable for everyone.

But to reach more people, I need your help.

Most people choose books based on reviews. So, I'm asking you to help someone else by leaving a review.

It costs nothing and takes less than a minute but could change someone's financial journey and turn around a family's future. Your review could help…

…one more family get out of debt
　…one parent build their emergency fund for their family
　…one child understand money to start their life out better than they started
　…one more person take control of their finances
　…one more dream come true

If you love helping others, you're my kind of person. Thank you from the bottom of my heart!

To make a difference, simply scan the QR code below, or click on the link and leave a review:

  https://amzn.to/4ecGFVe

Emma Maxwell

References

- *Understanding the Importance of Mindset in Financial ...* https://www.conovercompany.com/understanding-the-importance-of-mindset-in-financial-literacy/
- *Financial Literacy Helps Families Thrive* https://www.acf.hhs.gov/css/ocsevoiceblog/2021/04/financial-literacy-helps-families-thrive
- *How to Set S.M.A.R.T. Financial Goals (With Examples)* https://finmasters.com/smart-financial-goals/
- *Types of household budgets* https://www.aia.com/en/health-wellness/healthy-living/healthy-finances/household-budget-types
- *How to Create a Budget in 6 Simple Steps - Better Money Habits* https://bettermoneyhabits.bankofamerica.com/en/saving-budgeting/creating-a-budget
- *Best Budget Apps for Families (2024): 7 Tools to Manage Money at Home* https://marriagekidsandmoney.com/best-budget-apps-for-families/
- *10 Ways to Reduce Expenses* https://www.experian.com/blogs/ask-experian/how-to-reduce-expenses/
- *Easy Steps To Building an Emergency Fund on a Tight Budget* https://thedollarstretcher.com/personal-finance/ways-to-build-emergency-fund-on-tight-budget/
- *Secured Debt vs. Unsecured Debt: What's the Difference?* https://www.investopedia.com/ask/answers/110614/what-difference-between-secured-and-unsecured-debts.asp#:~:text=Secured%20loans%20require%20some%20sort,creditworthy%20in%20the%20lender's%20eyes.
- *This couple used the debt pay down method to pay off $130,000 in four years* https://www.nbcnews.com/better/lifestyle/couple-used-debt-snowball-

method-pay-130-000-four-years-ncna1059086
- *Debt Accelerator Method: What To Know and How To Start* https://www.lendingtree.com/debt-consolidation/debt-avalanche-method/
- *How to Get Out of Credit Card Debt: A 5-Step Guide* https://www.nerdwallet.com/article/finance/credit-card-debt
- *Invest in Their Future: A Guide to Family Financial Planning* https://www.investopedia.com/guide-to-family-financial-planning-8418295
- *Stocks, Bonds And Mutual Funds: Key Differences* https://www.bankrate.com/retirement/stocks-bonds-and-mutual-funds/
- *The Power of Compound Interest: Calculations and Examples* https://www.investopedia.com/terms/c/compoundinterest.asp
- *The Power Of Diversification: Building A Successful Family Business Strategy* https://aaronhall.com/the-power-of-diversification-building-a-successful-family-business-strategy/
- *Retirement Needs Worksheet* https://www.schwabmoneywise.com/resource/retirement-needs-worksheet
- *Retirement Income Calculator - Investor Vanguard* https://investor.vanguard.com/tools-calculators/retirement-income-calculator
- *Roth IRA vs. Traditional IRA* https://www.schwab.com/ira/roth-vs-traditional-ira
- *The power of compound growth in 401(k) plans* https://humaninterest.com/learn/articles/power-of-compound-growth-401k-plans/
- *Teaching Kids About Money: An Age-by-Age Guide* https://www.parents.com/parenting/money/family-finances/teaching-kids-about-money-an-age-by-age-guide/
- *21 Financial Literacy Games to Make Learning Fun - OppU* https://www.opploans.com/oppu/financial-literacy/games-financial-literacy/
- *Allowances and Kids: How to Build Health Habits Early* https://www.investopedia.com/guide-allowances-and-kids-5217591
- *How to start investing as a teenager* https://www.fidelity.com/learning-center/personal-finance/teach-teens-investing
- *Federal income tax rates and brackets - IRS* https://www.irs.gov/filing/federal-income-tax-rates-and-brackets#:~:text=You%20pay%20tax%20as

REFERENCES

%20a,rate%20on%20your%20entire%20income.
- *Roth IRA vs. 401(k): What's the Difference?* https://www.investopedia.com/ask/answers/100314/whats-difference-between-401k-and-roth-ira.asp
- *Tax-Loss Harvesting: Definition, How It Works* https://www.nerdwallet.com/article/taxes/tax-loss-harvesting
- *Child Tax Credit | Internal Revenue Service* https://www.irs.gov/credits-deductions/individuals/child-tax-credit#:~:text=Be%20under%20age%2017%20at,financial%20support%20during%20the%20year
- *The Psychology of Saving: Overcoming Barriers to Financial Success* https://www.rudowealth.com/rudo-blog-posts/the-psychology-of-saving-overcoming-barriers-to-financial-success
- *How to Develop a Positive Money Mindset* https://www.briantracy.com/blog/financial-success/how-to-develop-a-positive-money-mindset/
- *Money Fears Turned Money Success Story* https://www.myjourneytoinfluence.com/money-fears-turned-money-success-story/

www.ingramcontent.com/pod-product-compliance
Lightning Source LLC
Chambersburg PA
CBHW072212070526
44585CB00015B/1302